EDUCATIONAL VALUES AND IDEAS

SALMAN KHAN

ABSRTACT

INTRODUCTION

In the later part of 19th century four great contemporary Odia Litterateurs, namely, Radhanath Rai, Madhusudan Rao, Gangadhar Meher and Fakir Mohan Senapati played a commendable role not only for the upliftment and enrichment of Odia Language and literature but also contributed to the field of Education with new thoughts and ideas. Radhanath Rai and Madhusudan Rao worked in the department of education in different capacities and so they could contribute to the field of education. Fakir Mohan Senapati and Gangadhar Meher were not directly associated with the education of the time. However their contribution to the field of education cannot be ignored. The ideas on education contained in their literature are highly relevant and significant even in the present educational context. A number of researches have been conducted to study the educational contributions of Radhanath Rai and Madhusudan Rao, but so far no substantial research work has been conducted to evaluate the educational ideas present in the literature of Fakir Mohan Senapati. Yet the literature of Fakir Mohan Senapati contains invaluable philosophical educational ides, which need to be studies in proper perspective. Hence the present study

EDUCATIONAL VALUES AND IDEAS

The objectives of the study were :

i. To give an outline of Odisha during the time of Fakir Mohan Senapati (physical features, political scenario, social system, economic condition, cultural background and public instruction).

ii. To give a brief life sketch and philosophy of Fakir Mohan Senapati.

iii. To give a brief description of the literary works of Fakir Mohan Senapati so as to study the educational ideas contained in his literature in relation to:-

- Concept of education
- Aims of education
- Education is the instrument of social change
- Curriculum and method of instruction
- Women education

Nineteenth century renaissance in Odisha passed through the stages of reformations and enlightenment as elsewhere in renaissance history. Fakir Mohan Senapati an undaunted reformist made literature as his weapon to realize his aim of social reformation and political territorial unity of Odia speaking territories.

Deeply rooted to the culture of Odisha, Fakir Mohan Senapati in his reformist endeavor accommodated the traditional virtues in the indigenous culture and tradition and dispelled the evil practices which has made strong hold in to over culture because of lack of education and ignorance. Education, for Fakir Mohan Senapati was a means of realizing the society involving all the positive and negative aspect of it. Even if he had respect for the tradition and culture of Odisha, he did not oppose to integrate the western knowledge and education with cautions to resolve the conflict between the traditional and the modern.

Movement like feminism, women liberalization and women empowerment had been issues and that had become prominent in the west in the early decades of the nineteenth century. Fakir Mohan Senapati might not have been aware of such western movements but his personal wisdom was enough to make him realize that a healthy family and a healthy nation could be a reality only through women education and thus women empowerment. Greatly informed as a man of genius Fakir Mohan Senapati was not unaware of the great Indian tradition when women shared equal achievement in the field of knowledge and wisdom. It was a golden era of Indian society. Fakir Mohan, therefore, in many of his short stories in particular highlighted women education and rightful place for women in family and society so that his reformist and ideologies could be realized. The scholar has discussed at length the stories of Fakir Mohan Senapati highlighting women education. The novels of Fakir Mohan brought under discussion by the scholar shows how lack of education was responsible for the ignorance of people and made them victims of exploitation by the foreign and local exploiters.

CHAPTER WISE DESCRIPTION

The whole thesis has been divided into eight chapters.

Chapter **I** introduces the problem consisting of the relationship between literature and education deals with need and title of the study, scope and delimitation, objectives of the study and methodology. Analytic method based on intensive library research was adopted for the study.

Chapter **II** reviews the related literature available in the field. A review of all the four survey of research in education edited by M.B. Buch and the fifth survey of educational research edited by NCERT shows the number of research works have been conducted in the areas of educational thoughts and ideas present in great literary works. It also provides important information on methodological aspects. Further, studies conducted on different aspect on Fakir Mohan Senapati's life and literature, mostly by the scholars of Odia language and literature, reveal that no study has been conducted to analyze the educational ideas contain in the literature of Fakir Mohan Senapati.

Chapter **III** deals with Odisha during the time of Fakir Mohan Senapati – its physical features, political scenario, social system, economic condition, cultural background, public instruction, indigenous education and western education. Odisha during the time of Fakir Mohan Senapati was passing through a critical period. It was a name usually given to the geographical area dominated by the odia speaking people. Its territorial boundary was limited to Odisha division of the Bengal Presidency. Odisha was constituted of two geographical regions, namely, the coastal plains and the highlands featured by hills and forests. A frequent natural calamity was a prominent impeding feature of the physical design of Odisha. The people of Odisha were simple, conservative , superstitious, dogmatic and devoutly religious and priest ridden. There was severe social exploitation by the Zamindars, and petty officials and clerks under the government. However, the social reforms like the abolition of Sati and Child Marriage, Promotion of Women Education, Suppression of Mariah and infanticide, construction of roads and establishment of schools gradually started transforming the social life of the people. The rigorous caste system was whittled down by mass participation in the National Freedom Movement. During the period, the economy of Odisha was thoroughly deranged due to frequent drought and floods, over dependence on agriculture, faulty and revenue administration, lack of communication, non utilization of natural recourses and above all, misgoverance and the rapacious attitude of rulers. The culture of Odisha was identified with all the embracing Jagannath Culture. It was highly enriched by the Odishan and Chauhan style of architecture, Odissi Dance, and the dances and the songs of Tribal dominated western region of Odisha. The period was marked by renaissance of Odia Literature, Introduction of Printing Press, wide circulation of news Papers and books, and the role of Journalism ushering in new age of awakening Odisha. During the time of Fakir Mohan Senapati both indigenous and western education continued to co-exist in Odisha. There was a declining trend in the indigenous education system due to the inroad and gradual expansion of western education, However, the progress of education in general was much slower in the western hilly region of Odisha as compared to that in the coastal plains.

Chapter **IV** discusses the life sketch of Fakir Mohan Senapati – his family background, birth place, childhood, education and profession. This chapter also discusses Fakir Mohan as a teacher, a journalist, a social reformer, and an Administrator**.** Fakir Mohan's family life, poverty, character are also discussed in the Chapter.

Fakir Mohabn Senapati was born on Friday, the 14th of January 1843 or 1250 of the Sana era in the village of Malikashpur of Balasore. His father was Laxman Charan Senapati and mother, Tulsi Dei. After the death of his parents, he was brought up by his grandmother, Kochila Dei. The role of father and mother was played by his uncle Purusottama Senapati and his grandmother respectively. The name Fakir Mohan itself implies the fusion of both Muslim and Hindu communities. Besides that, his life is also a glaring example of Muslim impact on Hindu culture. John Bims getting well acquainted with Fakir Mohan's caliber insisted him to be the "Diwan" of Nilagiri. He served as the Diwan of Nilagiri from 1871 to 1875 at a monthly salary Rs.1,000/- after which he served as "Diwan" at various places of Odisha. He was Diwan at Damapada from 1876 to 1877, at Dhenkanal from 1877 to 1833, at Dasapalla from 1884 to 1886, at Pallahada from 1886 to 1887, at Keonjhar from 1887 to 1892, at Damapada for the second time from 1894 to 1896. He stayed at Cuttack from 1896 to 1905 and was associated with various literary institutions. He spent his last time at Balasore till death.

Chapter **V** deals with different novels and short stories of Fakir Mohan Senapati" When there is the bustle of progress of everywhere, will Utkal be still in slumber?" This line from Fakir Mohan's first original poem *Utkal Bhraman* (Tours of Odisha) not only epitomizes his literary overview but also depicts his flare for Odia nationalism. Fakir Mohan Senapati , regarded as the father of modern Odia literature, dedicated his entire life for the progress of Odia language. He also played a leading role in establishing the distinct identity of Odia language and literature. So the story of Fakir Mohan is indeed the story of "renaissance" in Odia literature. Fakir Mohan's autobiography "*Atma Jiban Charita*" is not only the first of its kind in Odia but remains the best and most interesting in India languages. Moreover, it is as readable as any of his novels and exciting short-stories. *Vyasa Kavi's* novels are *Chhamana Atha guntha* (1902), *Lachhama* (1903) , *Mamu* (1913), and *Prayaschita* (1915). Fakir Mohan is considered as the greatest prose writer in Odia literature. But it is amazing to note that he hardly wrote any prose until he retired from administrative service. He translated Ramayan, Mahabharat and some of the Upanishads from the original Sanskrit for which he is popularly known as *Vyasa Kavi*. He wrote poetry too, but the themes of his poem were not considered conventionally fit for poetry. He used colloquial, spoken and rugged language of the common man, which no poet in Odia had done for centuries. Fakir Mohan wrote four novels, two volumes of short-stories and one autobiography. He mastered the art of writing short stories for which he is also termed as *Katha Samrat* (Emperor of Shortstories)in Odia literature. Fakir Mohan gave a new spirit and vigor to Odia novels of his time. His novels were written on the hard and stark reality of his contemporary society. He introduced the problematic social novels instead of romantic and historical novels. It would not be an exaggeration to say that he ushered in an epoch-making era in Odia novel writing and also contributed to the growth of Indian Fiction writing.

Chapter **VI** explores Fakir Mohan's Philosophy of life , a believer in God, a staunch idealist, a lover of nature, a humanist and a nationalist. Fakir Mohan Senapati's literary creations, experiences of life and correspondence with his contemporaries reveal his philosophy of life. His philosophy is deep-rooted in Indian idealism and spiritualism. Fakir Mohan Senapati was a believer in God. He believed god as the ultimate reality and surrendered his ego to Him. He regarded God as the Universal Soul. Fakir Mohan Senapati emphasized on devotion and self-less dedication to humanity to realize God. Idealism formed the base of Fakir Mohan Senapati's life and literature. As an idealist Fakir Mohan Senapati led a life based on simple living and high thinking. He believed in certain ideals and principles, and lived to up hold and glorify those ideals. Fakir Mohan Senapati was a strong lover of nature. He personified Nature by injecting life into it and emphasized on the great virtue of educating human society through nature. In Fakir Mohan Senapati's subtle vision, Nature is always sympathetic to human cause. According to him , nature is a tested friend and solace giver, and equally shares human emotions like sorrows and happiness. Fakir Mohan was a great humanist. Through his innumerable literary creations he tried to inform , educate and enlighten people about the noble virtues of humanism. He believed in the fatherhood of God and brotherhood of man. Fakir Mohan's creations reflect his desire for a human society based on justice, equality, fraternity, secularism and other democratic principles. He voiced his resentment against exploitation of innocent illiterate and rural masses.

Chapter **VII** explores the educational ideas contained in the literature of Fakir Mohan Senapati. It deals with the Concept of education, Aims of education, education as the instrument of social change, Curriculum and Method of Instruction, Women education and various other aspects of education. Although not an educationalist himself, Fakir Mohan Senapati has thrown light on various aspects of education through his vast literary works. Fakir Mohan Senapati has defined education as a lifelong process. Education does not end in school. He has treated the whole world as the field of education. According to him education refines the feelings of heart. Fakir Mohan Senapati has categorized people into three groups; educated, uneducated and pseudo-educated. Although Fakir Mohan Senapati has not expressed his views exclusively on curriculum, and methods of instruction, his literature suggests a broad and comprehensive school curriculum. Fakir Mohan Senapati's literature suggests that the school curriculum should include literature, grammar, composition, history, civics, geography, culture, science, vocational subject like agriculture and dairy farming, physical training, aesthetic education, religious education and nature study. Fakir Mohan Senapati has realized the role of women in the society as inevitable, and has introduced powerful women characters in his literary works. He has tried to build up their characters with good education. He was in favour of the spread of women education based on Indian culture. His literature suggests that religious education, moral education, discipline, lesson on management of family affairs and upbringing of children and home science to be the content of women education. Fakir Mohan Senapati's literature reflects his views in favour of free and compulsory education. In order to make it a reality, Fakir Mohan Senapati has stressed on quantitative expansion of education. He has also advocated for adult education to provide functional literacy to the illiterate peasants. He has appealed to them to work in the day and learn in the night. Fakir Mohan Senapati has put emphasis on child psychology in the process of education. Fakir Mohan Senapati's philosophy of education not only makes a harmonious blending of different philosophy of education, but also has the imprints of the thoughts of the great Indian educationists who have brought fresh light in the field of education.

Chapter **VIII** consists of summary, conclusion and recommendation. The summary of the previous chapters are briefly presented. The conclusion and recommendations are for further studies.

Table with regard to Values in Fakir Mohan's novels and short stories

Sl.No.	Name of the Novels	Year of Publication	Values
1	Chha Mana Atha Guntha	1897-1899 (Utkal Sahitya Patrika & as a Novel in 1902)	Educational, Social & Ethical value
2	Lachhama	1903	Educational, Social & Historical value
3	Mamu	1913	Educational, Social & Ethical value
4	Prayaschita	1915	Educational, Social & Ethical value

Sl. No.	Name of the Story	Name of magazine in which published	Month & Year of Publication	Values
1	Lachhamania	Bodhadayini	1868(not available)	------
2	Rebati	Utkal Sahitya 2nd part, 10th number	October 1898	Social & educational value
3	Mauna Mauni	Mukura, 2nd part 2nd number	May 1907	Ethical value
4	Baleswari Rahajani	Mukura, 2nd part 4th number	July 1907	Social & ethical value

5	Baleswari Panga Luna	Mukura, 2nd part 6th number	September 1907	Social value
6	Punar Musika Bhaba	Mukura, 4th part 1st & 2nd number	April, May 1909	Educational value
7	Daaka Munsi	Mukura, 7th part 6th number	September 1912	Social, Ethical & Educational value
8	Dhulia Baba	Utkal Sahitya 16th part, 11th number	February 1913	Social & Educational value
9	Kamala Prasad Goraap	Utkal Sahitya 17th part, 2nd number	May 1913	Educational value
10	Sunaa Bahu	Utkal Sahitya 17th part, 3rd number	June 1913	Educational & Social value
11	Raandipua Anantaa	Mukura, 8th part 4th number	July 1913	Social, Ethical & Educational value
12	Kaalika Prasad Gorap	Utkal Sahitya 17th part, 5th number	August 1913	Social & Ethical value
13	Patent Medicine	Utkal Sahitya 17th part, 6th number	September 1913	Social, Ethical & Educational value
14	Beerei Bishala	Utkal Sahitya 17th part, 7th number	October 1913	Social Education value
15	Sabhya Jamidar	Utkal Sahitya 17th part, 12th number	March 1914	Social & Ethical value
16	Bagala Baguli	Utkal Sahitya 18th part, 1st number	April 1914	Ethical & Educational value
17	Ajaa Nati Katha	Utkal Sahitya 19th part, 1st number	April 1915	Social & Educational value
18	Pathoi Bahu	Mukura, 10th part 3rd number	June 1915	Educational & Ethical value
19	Adharma Bitta	Utkal Sahitya 19th part, 5th number	August 1915	Social Educational value
20	Madha Mohantynka Kanya Suna	Utkal Sahitya 19th part, 7th number	October 1915	Social & Ethical value
21	Gaarudi Mantra	Utkal Sahitya 20th part, 8th number	November 1916	Social & Educational value

CONCLUSION

Like any other idealistic thinker, Fakir Mohan Senapati has contributed more to enrich the aim of education than the curriculum or the method of instruction. Glorification of the mother tongue and motherland get top priority in Fakir Mohan's consideration, which seem relevant even today. Nevertheless, Fakir Mohan's vast literature presents a critical appreciation of the highly rich Indian tradition and customs. The protagonists of his long narratives demonstrate living examples of the dos and don'ts of social virtues. The numerous educational ides present in the literature of Fakir Mohan constitute a major source of informal mass education. It is quite common among the masses in Odisha that they do not forget to quote some educative lines from the popular Odia poets to help solve social discord and to explain and establish their arguments in social situations. The socio-linguistic skill is not limited to the literates only. Thus Fakir Mohan Senapati occupies the first position among his equals due to the oriental inclination of his characters in nourishing a tradition of informal education. It is needless to say that the educative lines from Fakir Mohan Senapati's literature should draw the attention of the curriculum framers and policy planners in the field of education in Odisha.

CHAPTER-I

INTRODUCTION

CHAPTER-I

INTRODUCTION

1.1 LITERATURE AND EDUCATION

The Advanced Learner's Dictionary of Current English lays down the meaning of literature and pieces of writing that are valued as works of arts, especially novels, plays and pieces of writing or printed information on a particular subject.[1] Literature is a medium of self- expression. It is the artistic form of individual's feeling expressed through language. It symbolizes immortality. Literature is universal as well it is not confined to any nation, race or time. It belongs to the entire human race and is based on human problems. Literature is sweet and useful, and it provides aesthetic pleasure to man. It has the power to attract the mind, vitality and consciousness. "Literature is the source of truth, goodness and beauty.[2]

Literature is as old as human civilization. It provides a detailed account of the happenings in different walks of life. 'Literature contains varied elements starting from politics and diplomacy to science, commerce, sports, entertainment, logic and everything.[3] Literary works are treasures of knowledge. Through them we can look back to the distant past and also have a vision for the future. As rightly observed by P.C Mohanty, literature is not only the description of what has already happened but also what can happen or what is the possibility in future.[4] In literature, Rabindranath Tagore discovered a feeling of union between man and man, past and present, far and near.[5] The traditional literature helps by bridging the gap between the past and the present. It helps in transferring the knowledge, experience, customs and traditions from one generation to another. The relationship between literature and life is very intimate. Plato rightly described "literature as an imitation of life".[6] For Mathew Arnold it is the criticism of life.[7] Hudson termed it as fundamentally an expression of life through the medium of language.[8] R. J. Reese stated, It as a permanent expression of some thought or feeling of idea about life and the world.[9] Shelley defined, "literature as the very image of life expressed in its eternal truth".[10] Thus literature is always life oriented and its scope is as broad and unlimited as life. Literature increases our knowledge to understand human life and the world. It provides abundant clues to solve the various problems of life. Literature analyses the real life and shows direction for an ideal living.[11] It gives perfection to life.

Literature represents life and life to a great extent is a social reality. Literature is directly related to the society. It reflects a clear picture of the contemporary society, highlighting on the intimacy between literature and society. B.K. Nanda states that," literature is a social institution. It is the manifestation of the society". Literature himself/herself is a social being and has a social responsibility. A Literature should be a representative of his time and his society. A good Literature does not write as per the prevailing social system only. He also attempts to reform the society by creating his own group of readers and fans.[12] Further P.C. Mohanty rightly observes that, literature aims at social welfare improves human relations, gives moral direction and guides man and society to choose appropriate path. The entire society and its activities and problems form the content of literature.[13] In this context, U.S. Singh States that, "literature influences, entertains and directly or indirectly benefits the society".[14] Literature brings in desirable changes in the attitude and behaviour of people. It has a deep socio-cultural root. On the one hand it is always influenced by the society and on the other, it keeps on influencing the society by informing, entertaining, educating and propagating the thoughts and ideas of the time. Literature expresses the entire aspirations of the society.

Keeping in view its intimacy with the people, literature proves to be a powerful agency of education. Rabindranath Tagore justifiably treated literature as the true vehicle of education. He advised for the study of literature for cultural significance and for the study of mass Psychology.[15]

Literature contains moral values and satisfies man's need for moral instruction combined with entertainment.

Literature creates a high degree of interest and makes learning more permanent. It contains highly educative values and proves to be a good source of value education. There exists a very close relationship between literature and education as it is between literature and society. This relationship can be compared with the relationship between philosophy and education as well. According to J.S. Ross, philosophy and education, like two sides of a coin, present different views of the same thing, and that, one is implied by the other.[17] Both literature and education aim at bringing desirable changes in the attitude and behavior of the individuals. We find an intimate interconnection of literature, philosophy and education. Both the philosophical and educational ideas are reflected in literature. Again, a person presents his views on education through literature. Literature, thus, may be called, the mother of philosophy of education. It is literature, which reflects ideas, and most of the ideas at core are educational. Literature, like philosophy, gives direction to education. Thus education can also be termed as the dynamic side of literature.

The great classics in world literature are the greatest pieces of education, and the great literary figures may truly be termed as the great educationists. There are many examples. Starting from the Vedic Rishis through Kalidas, Shakespeare Tolstoy to Rabindranath Tagore and Sri Aurobindo – all were great educationists. All of them have left invaluable pieces of advice and have been instrumental in awakening and educating the masses. Study of a piece of literature not only gives pleasure to our mind but it guides our every step by providing direction to our belief, values knowledge, attitude, culture and even vocations of life. Researches conducted in the field reveal the fact that literature has been considered as one of the major areas of educational research. Reiterating the significance of educational researches on literature, Govind Rao (1955) points out that knowledge exists in the soul of literature.[18] Such studies are significant as they attempt to explore some general principles connecting literature and educational system. Hence a literary piece should be studied intensively to find out the educational ideas of the time, which is supposed to contribute to the world of knowledge in the field of education.

1.2 NEED AND TITLE OF THE STUDY:-

In the later part of 19th Century, Odia language and literature was confronted with the dangers of extinction. At that critical juncture some great personalities took up their pens and rose to the occasion to rescue it from the crisis. Those great litterateurs who relentlessly struggled for the upliftment and enrichment of Odia language and literature were Gangadhar Meher, Radhanath Ray, Madhusudan Rao and last but not the least Fakir Mohan Senapati. Among them Fakir Mohan Senapati was more a writer of prose- fictions and novels whereas the rest three were poets of eminence. They introduced new styles and techniques to the literary trends of the time. Their efforts deserve high commendation and appreciation not only for the development of Odia language and literature, but also for the thoughts and ideas contributed to the field of education. These four great figures of Odisha contributed to the field of education in their own unique style. Radhanath Rai and Madhusudan Rao were working in the department of education in different capacities and therefore, they contributed deliberately and practically to the field of education. Though Fakir Mohan Senapati and Gangadhar Meher were not directly associated with the education of the time, their contribution to the theory of education cannot be ignored. The educational ideas contained in their literature are of high relevance and significance in the present educational context.

A number of researches have been conducted to study the educational contribution of Gopabandhu Dash, Fakir Mohan Senapati, Radhanath Rai and Madhusudan Rao, but so far no substantial research work has been conducted to evaluate the educational ideas present in the literature of Fakir Mohan Senapati, except a few piece-meal studies. The literature of Fakir Mohan Senapati reflects invaluable philosophical and educational ideas, which are pregnant with direct teachings on vocational education and value education. All these need to be studied in proper perspectives. Moreover the educational idea of Fakir Mohan Senapati is very much relevant and useful to the modern educational system. His ideas can provide solutions to the problems faced by the present-day education system in India. Hence, realizing the urgent need to conduct a comprehensive study on the educational ideas present in the literature of Odia poet Fakir Mohan Senapati, the researcher undertook the study titled:

"EDUCATIONAL VALUES AND IDEAS CONTAINED IN THE LITERATURE OF FAKIR MOHAN SENAPATI"

1.3 SCOPE AND DELIMITATION OF THE STUDY.

Fakir Mohan Senapati has a vast literature to his credit, both published and unpublished. The present study includes only the published work highlighting those portions, which contain his educational and philosophical ideas and ideals. The main source of the present study is Fakir Mohan Granthavali (Collection of Fakirmohan's literary works).It also covers the study of contemporary authors' writings that throw light on the educational ideas of Fakir Mohan Senapati. In addition to that the present study includes the study of letters, correspondences, and experiences collected from sources close to Fakir Mohan Senapati to get a clear picture about the poet's philosophical and educational ideas.

1.4 OBJECTIVES OF THE STUDY

The objectives of the present study are stated as follows:-

i) To give an outline of Odisha during the time of Fakir Mohan Senapati (physical features, political scenario, social system, economic condition, cultural background and public instruction)

ii) To give a brief life sketch and philosophy of Fakir Mohan Senapati.

iii) To give a brief description of the literary works of Fakir Mohan Senapati so as to study the educational ideas contained in his literature with relation to :

- Concept of education

- Aims of education

- Curriculum and method of instruction

- Women education

1.5 METHODOLOGY

The surveys on education research indicate that for studies on educational ideas/thoughts/contributions/philosophy of individual thinkers the methods that the researchers have employed have been variously described as historical, library research, descriptive, analytical, and comparative and content analysis. They have used for their studies literature available in the form of books, primary and secondary sources, personal interview, visits to institutions, old records, commentaries, speeches and writings.[19] Thus historical method, library method, biographical method etc, are just different names given to the methods of philosophical inquiry. All these methods adopt similar exercise of gathering information from the sources, critically analyzing and classifying them, and drawing conclusion on the basis of critical analysis. As the topic under investigation is also a philosophical inquiry, the researcher has adopted source analysis method based on intensive library research. Thus the present study is an analytical research. The researcher has to use facts or information already available, and analyze these to make a critical evaluation of the material.[20] The present study is also rational and not empirical. According to Roadman and Sherman, rationalistic studies are conducted through qualitative methods where as empirical studies are conducted through quantitative methods.[21] The present study thus involves qualitative approach. For the present study materials have been collected from both primary and secondary sources. The relevant literature of Fakir Mohan Senapati, his letters, correspondence, and experience collected from sources close to him various official records and reports of committees and commissions relating to education, and gazetteers were taken as primary sources of data. Other sources like books, journals, periodicals, newspaper, literary criticisms and published and unpublished research woks were also consulted for the present study. Records from the Archives and Regional Archive of Odia were consulted. The collected data have been carefully taken and discussed on the basis of the set objectives. The books and documents consulted for the study are enlisted in the bibliography.

REFERENCES

1. Advanced learners Dictionary of Current English, Oxford, 2000, P.751

2 R.C. Samantray, Sahityashree" The Samaj, Cuttack, Date 15.11.1998, P.21

3. B.P. Mahapatra, Matrubhasa Odia, Cuttack: Friends Publishers, 1997, P.21

4. P.C Mohanty, Sahityara Sambidhana, Sambalpur : Saraswat Book Store, 1998, P 43

5 Ibid P4

6 Ibid p432

7 Ibid p2

8 Ibid p2

9 Ibid p2

10 Ibid p 45

11 RC Samabtaray, op.cit.

12 B. K. Nansada, "Sahitya O Samaja", The Samaj, Cuttack, Date 19.02.1995, P.7

13 P.C. Mohanty, op.cit., PP. 58-59

14 U.S. Singh, "Meher Sahityrara Samajika Angikarabaddhata", The Pragativadi, Bhubaneswar, Date 05.09.1999.

15 B.N.Dash, Principles of Education and Education in the Emerging Indian Society, Delhi : Ajanta Publication, 1982, P.125

16 P.C. Mohanty, op.cit., p-28

17. I.S. Ross, Ground Work of Educational Theory, London : George G. Harrap and Co.Ltd., 1942, P.11

18 M.B Buch(ed.), A Survey of Research in Education, Baroda : CASE (Sponsored by NCERT, New Delhi), 1974, p.37

19 M. B. Buch (ed.), Fourth Survey of Research in Education (1983-1988), Vol.- New Delhi : NCERT, 1991, P. 5

20 C. R. Kothari, Research Methodology : Methods and Techniques, New Delhi : Wiley Eastern Limited, 1990, P.3

21 W.B. Roadman and R.R. Sherman, Qualitative Research in Education: Focus and Methods, London : The Falmer Press , 1988. P.11

♦♦♦

CHAPTER-II

REVIEW OF RELATED LITERATURE

CHAPTER II

REVIEW OF RELATED LITERATURE

The review of related literature forms an important step in the research process as it promotes greater understanding of the researches already conducted in the same field over a period of time, highlights the strengths and weaknesses of the previous studies so as to enable the researcher to improve his own study, helps to eliminate duplication and serves as guidepost to take new strides in the field for furtherance of knowledge. Review of related literature also acquaints the researcher with the latest knowledge available in the field of her research, helps to state the objectives clearly and concisely and gives an understanding of the method of the study. According to C.R. Kothari, related studies indicate possible difficulties and analytical shortcomings that may be encountered in the present study, and at time suggest useful and even new lines of approach to the present problem.[1]

The history of Odia Literature has been mapped by historians and linguists along the following stages: Old on Ancient Odia (900-1300 AD), Early Middle Odia (1300-1500 AD), Middle Odia (1500-1700 AD), Late Middle Odia (1700 AD-1850 AD) and Modern Odia (from 1850 AD till the present). But this rude categorization could not skillfully draw the real picture on account of development and growth of Odia Literature. Here, we split the total periods in different stages such as: Age of Charya Literature (14th Century), Age of Sarala Das (15th Century), Age of Panchasakha (16th century to 1650), Age of Madhya Yuga (1650-1880), and Age of Modern (1880- till today). Modern Age devided into below ways like-Radhanath Age (1880-1910), Satyabadi Age (1910-1921), Sabuja Age (1921-1935), Pragati Age (1936-1946), Altra Modern Age or Post Independent Age (1946 –till today) etc.

The beginning of Odia poetry coincides with the development of Charya Sahitya, the literature started by Mahayana Buddhist poets. This literature was written in a specific metaphor named "Sandhya Bhasha" and the poets like Luipa, Kanhupa are from the territory of Odisha. The language of Charya was considered as Prakrita. The first great poet of Odisha is the famous Sarala Das who wrote the Mahabharata, not an exact translation from the Sanskrit original, rather an imitation of the same. Among many of his poems and epics, he is best remembered for his Mahabharata. Chandi Purana and the Vilanka Ramayana are also two of his famous creations. Arjuna Das, a contemporary to Sarala Das, wrote Rama-Bibha, a significant long poem in Odia. Towards the 16th century, five poets emerged over a period of one hundred years. They are known as Panchashakhas as they believed in the same school of thought the Utkaliya Vaishnavism. The poets are Balaram Das, Jagannath Das, Achyutananada Das, Ananta Das and Jasobanta Das. In 1509 Chaitanya Jaydev had prepared the ground by heralding the cult of Vaishnavism through his Geetagovinda. Chaitanya's path of devotion was known as Raganuga Bhakti Marga. The Panchasakhas differed from Chaitanyas and believed in Gyana Mishra Bhakti Marga, which had similarities with the Buddhist philosophy of Charya Literature stated above. After the age of Panchasakhas, the prominent poets were Dinakrushna Das, Upendra Bhanja and Abhimanyu Samanta Simhar. Verbal jugglery, obscenity and eroticism were the characteristics of Shringara Kavyas. They became the trends of this period to which Upendra Bhanja took a leading role. His literary creations 'Baidehisha Bilasa', 'Koti Brahmanda Sundari', 'Lavanyabati' proved land mark in odia Literature. Upendra Bhanja was conferred on with the title 'Kabi Samrat' of odia literature for his aesthetic poetic sense and proficient verbal jugglery. Dinakrushna Das's 'Rasokallola' and Abhimanyu Samanta Simhara's 'Bidagdha Chintamani' were prominent kavyas of this time. The first odia printing type-set was set up in 1836 by the Christian missionaries who made great contribution towards the growth of Odia literature through publication of books, journals and periodicals. The first odia Magazine of 'Bodha Dayini' was published from Balasore in 1861. The main object of this magazine was to promote odia literature and to draw attention to the lapses in government policy. The first Odia Newspaper, 'The Utkal Deepika' made its appearance in 1866 under the editorship of late Gouri Sankar Ray with the help of late Bichitrananda. The publication of these papers during the last part of the 19th century encouraged the modern literature and acted as a medium to provide a wide range of readers for the writers. The educated intellectuals came in contact with the English Literature and got influenced. Radhanath Ray (1849-1908) was the prime figure, who tried to write his poems under the influence of Western literature. His 'Chandrabhaga', 'Nandikeshwari','Usha','Mahajatra','Darbr' and 'Chilika' were long poems or Kavyas. Fakir Mohan Senapati (1843-1918), the prime figure of modern Odia prose fiction was the product of that generation. He was considered the Vyasakabi or founder story teller in Odia language. Fakir Mohan Senapati was known for his novel 'Chha Maana Atha Guntha'. It was among the first Indian novels to deal with the exploitations of landless peasants by the feudal lords.

Keeping in view with the above facts, a review of related literature concerning the present problem was conducted which has been presented in the following paragraphs under two sections, namely, (1) educational studies based on literary works in general, (ii) studies conducted on the works of Fakir Mohan senapati. The studies have been presented in chronological order.

2.1 EDUCATIONAL STUDIES BASED ON LITERARY WORKS IN GENERAL

A review of related studies shows that many researches have been conducted in the area of educational thoughts and ideas present in great literary works. Some of the worth-mentioning researches are reported here.

Govind Rao (1955)[2] studied the English novelists and their views on education. The objective of the study was to bring into light the thoughts on education present in the writings of different novelists like Jane Austin, Charles Dickens, D. Thomas, Samuel Butler, Yeats, George Meredith, Thomas Hardy, Arnold Bennett, John Goldworth, H.G. Wells and Virginia Wolf. The researcher adopted library research technique and analyzed the writings of the novelists. In the overall study, he reveals that education has been an important consideration to the novelists and it is an established truth that knowledge exists in the soul of literature.

Divekar (1960)[3] critically analised the educational philosophy of Upanishads. He concludes that according to Upanishads the teacher should be a man of character, integrity and developed personality so as to become an idol and ideal for the pupils, He should also foster the creativity and the spirit of inquiry of the pupils. He added that the Upanishad consisted of Para and Apara Vidya and that concentration of mind was supposed to be the keynote of all learning. The researcher recommended that the important features of educational philosophy in the Upanishads could be incorporated in modern educational system in India.

Charlu (1971)[4] discussed the educational philosophy of the Bhagavat Gita. It was a study of the philosophical aspects of the Gita with a view to forming a basis for the reconstruction of a sound educational system. Library research method was adopted for the study. The sources examined were Bhagavad Gita, commentaries on the Gita by various scholars, books on eastern and western philosophy along with research literature on the problem. The findings were reported as: (i) Education is found to mean the complete development of man through the four successive stages of life and the preparation for the present life and life after death. It connects an exercise of hand, head and heart with a view to developing a synthesis of matter and spirit. (ii) The educative process is a harmonious development of physique, intellect, social efficiency and character. (iii) Education insists on the cooperation of both the teacher and the pupil to gain knowledge of the supreme. The qualities of the teacher and the taught are the basic constituents of teacher-pupil relationship. (iv) The curriculum presented in the Gita contains the entire life and its problems as one subject. (v) Gita holds the thesis that knowledge and selfless action are the ways to serve God. Finally a comparative study of the educational philosophies of the Gita, the Bible and the Koran has been suggested.

Jha (1973)[5] examined the educational implications of Kamayani- an epic written by Jayasankar Prasad. The investigator has tried to show the relationship of this epic with old Sanskrit literature that has presented principles of educational importance allegorically. On the background of the gloom, which is pervading the present day life, the poet has tried to seek solutions through Kamayani. The poet has suggested that through education an effort should be made to produce balanced young men and women whose spiritual powers are developed in harmony with their mental power.

Sharma (1976)[6] analysed the essentials of education from the literature of the Jainism. It was a library study. Books on Jain philosophy and history formed the main sources of information. Buddhist literature was also referred to substantiate the information. The significant findings of the study were: (i) Although the Jain system of education had no big university, the centers of Jain pilgrimage, maths and vihars acted as centers of learning (ii) Salvation was considered as the ultimate aim of education. (iii) The Jain education system was multi-dimensional and education was regarded a lifelong process. (iv) The monitorial system was the contribution of Jain system of education (v) In Jain system education was subservient to religion.

Venkateswarlu (1978)[7] studied the educational philosophy as reflected in the Mahabharata. The method adopted was a critical examination of some of the salient situations and significant incidents of Mahabharata so as to highlight the right and efficacious human conduct, the conduct of parents, the conduct of teachers and the conduct of the government. Some of the major findings were: (i) The cultivation of virtues and a proper code of conduct were considered more important than the achievement of skills or advancement in the cognitive domain. (ii) Sacrifice as a means of creation was a law of nature and also a law of God. (iii) The Sankhya Philosophy of life was most suited to India as her national educational philosophy (iv) Varna was not by genes, it was by the qualities of head, heart and conduct. The division of labour was for efficiency. (v)The disciplines of food and dress were essential for educators and the educands. (vi) The intellect that had undergone sublimation, the Vadas, the functional Brahmin and the love of God were the effective sources of knowledge (vii) Parables, lively investigation, practical demonstration and pupil involvement in projects were the actual methods of education.

Dubey (1980)[8] evaluated the educational philosophy in Upanishads. This is the second study on Upanishads after Divekar (1960). The study adopted the historical cum-critical method and the necessary data were collected through extensive library work. The study revealed that: (i) The Upanishadic philosophy of education aimed at arousing the spiritual vision of human beings. It also aimed at developing character, truthfulness and proficiency in several worldly subjects for livelihood (ii) Education was open for all castes, creeds and women irrespective of their socio-economic status. (iii) Generally the duration of the study was twelve years. (iv) The entire educational system was residential. (v) The size of the class was five to six students (vi) Gurukulas were substantially added by the kings and landlords but they had no control on the educational policy and on the gurukulas. (vii) Education was free at all stages. (viii) The curriculum mainly consisted of two parts, *para vidya* (Subjects related to spiritual development) and *apara vidya* (Subjects like the Vedas, The Purana, grammar, social customs, mathematics, production, ethics, logic, geography,. Military science. Aesthetics, architecture, science, (ix) The teacher pupil relationship was extremely cordial and the teacher behaved like a father. (x) The methodology of teaching were hearing, contemplation, discussion, and question-answer. Formulation, debate, and inductive and deductive logic, explaining illustrating with examples, experimentation and learning by doing. (xi) The practice of acquired knowledge was immensely emphasized.

Biswal (1989)[9] made a study on the contributions of Radhanath Rai and Madhusudan Rao to the 19th Century educational situation in Odia. The objectives of the study were : (i) To provide a brief outline of 19th century Odisha physical features, history, economic condition, the socio-cultural scenario) (ii) To briefly describe the legacy of the decaying indigenous educational system that was getting supplanted by the western system of education. (iii) To outline the evolution of educational administration in the Bengal Presidency with special reference to the Odisha division from 1813 to 1912 (iv) To briefly describe the development of modern education in Odisha during the period from 1813 to 1912. (v) To highlight the role of Radhanath Rai as an educationist and litterateur (vi) To highlight the role of Madhusudan Rao as an educationist and litterateur. The source method was adopted for the study. The study gave special emphasis to Radhanath Rai's life, literary writings and contributions to the field of education as an inspecting officer and textbook writer. The study also emphasized on Madhusudan Rao's life, literature and contributions for the qualitative and quantitative improvement of schools in Odisha. As a teacher and inspecting officer Madhusudan Rao greatly contributed for the qualitative improvement of schools, and advocated the concept of life-long education, self-development scheme of teachers and co-curricular activities, and authored text books and books on pedagogy. The study was a humble tribute to the heroic educational endeavours of the two great stalwarts in the trying circumstances of nineteenth century of Odisha. This study assumes significance for the present study as Radhanath and Madhusudan were contemporaries to Fakir Mohan Senapati.

Prabhune (1990)[10] critically analysied Sane Guruji's literature to identify the educational values and objectives and to explore its educational philosophy. The methodology involved was the analytical study of Sane Guruji's literature and criticisms there on, supplemented by a study of the writings and interviews with persons known to Sane Guruji or acquainted with his work. A questionnaire was also used to find out the influence of Sane Guruji's literature in the minds of adolescent. Some major findings of the study were:(i)Every thing is based on the foundation of love. A teacher cannot teach successfully without love. The basic values-love, knowledge and power-are needed for living successfully, (ii) Sane Guruji's literature's sociological aspect depicts his generous attitude towards the poor, the oppressed, the untouchables and the workers, (iii) Each individual should get an opportunity to receive education of his/her expectation. The education system which gives an opportunity to the child to develop his personality is the best system. (iv) According to Sane Guruji, to sow the seeds of truth and reality and develop moral values with them is education (v) Sane Guruji accepts nature as a great teacher. (vi) According to the principles of vardhu sikshya, Sane Guruji emphasized on productivity, dignity of labour, virtues, research ability etc. (vii) According to Sane Guruji education should be well woven for character building. The findings did not point out what the questionnaire information revealed. They were just general pronouncements of different aspects of education by Sane Guruji.

Lohakare (1991)[11] discussed the educational philosophy in Samartha Ramdas Swamy's book Shri Dasbodha. The objectives were (i) to critically analyse the educational philosophy of Samarth Ramdas as depicted in Shri Dashodha, and ((ii) to find out the position of inclusion of the educational ideas contained in Shri Dasbodha in the curriculum of Marathi from class V to X and the utility of the educational philosophy in the curriculum. The study was based on the literature analysis supplemented by interviews of followers of the Shri Dasbodha literature. The major findings of the study were:

(1) *The values cherished by Samarth Ramdas:*

(a) Personal values selflessness, industriousness, simplicity, self-evaluation ability, self-control, purity, leadership, judiciousness, faith in science, efforts, rationality

(b) Social values-comprehensiveness equality, friendship, sacrifice, secularism

(c) Moral values-responsibility, truthfulness, sympathy and love for nature

(d) Spiritual values-faith in God, indifference, love and aesthetic attitude.

(2) Educational philosophy depicted in Shri Dasbodha includes spiritualism, realism, pragmatism and naturalism

(3) The study found reflection of certain elements of the educational philosophy of Shri Dasbodha in moral and spiritual values recommended by various committees and commissions.

Boulton (1993)[12] made a study titled Fakir Mohan Senapati : His life and Prose-fictions. The study was divided into two parts. The fourth chapter of the second part of the study highlighted the theme of education contained in Fakir Mohan's prose-fictions. They are: (i) Fakir Mohan Senapati expressed his dissatisfaction with western education as it produced educated elite, and it alienated this elite from its own society and culture. In Fakir Mohan's view, an elite educated in an alien tongue was of little value to the nation as a whole. (ii) Fakir Mohan, in his scheme of education, emphasized on patriotism and the traditional teacher-taught relationship. (iii) To Fakir Mohan, education meant being trained to behave with intelligence.

Education should not be merely vocational training, but a means of stimulating intellectual growth so that from infancy children could tackle the various problems of life with intelligence (iv) Fakir Mohan Senapati emphasized on the need for education as an antidote to superstition and as a protection against exploitation. (v) The initial step in the education of children should be to educate mothers. (vi) The education or training of mother in Orissa should not be the mere inculcation of traditional housewifely virtues. They should also be taught intelligent behaviour. Women should benefit from education in acquiring the ability to manage their affairs in the absence of a husband or a son. Fakir Mohan demonstrated in his thesis that, whilst a little education was a desirable thing in a woman, it should not take precedence over her traditional training as a housewife and mother, otherwise domestic unrest was inevitable.

2.2 STUDIES CONDUCTED ON THE WORKS OF FAKIR MOHAN SENAPATI.

A number of studies have been conducted on Fakir Mohan Senapati and his literature. Most of the studies were conducted by the scholars of the faculty of Odia language and literature. Some of them bearing the philosophical and educational ideas of Fakir Mohan Senapati have been reviewed and presented in the following paragraphs.

Nandini reveals in his book that [13] in "Laxmi Puran" he has given a higher place to woman than man where Goddess Laxmi had punished Lord Jagannath and Lord Balavadra for disapproving her closeness with a low-caste devotee. But it was an exception. During the period of Fakirmohan Senapati, we find woman in a new light. She can be courageous if necessary, and can beat her husband to reform him. But then she also serves him after he is beaten (Patent Medicine) in his works we find two types of woman, traditional and modern. The grandmother of Rebati, the wife of Zamidar are traditional, because they believe in tradition, conventions and superstitions. But there is also Rebati who wants to be educated and so she is modern.

Odia literature from a practical point of view is considered to have emerged with the great epic poem, the Mahabharata (1470 AD) by Sarala Das whose women characters were impressive. Fakirmohan Senapati was the pioneer of the modern Odia fiction. During the last hundred years after Fakir Mohan there have been a number of brilliant fiction writers in Odisha like Gopinath Mohanty, Surendra Mohanty, Kalandi Charan Panigrahi, Kanhu Charan Mohanty, Santanu Acharya and Pratibha Ray. Gopinath Mohanty, a classical artist, excels his contemporary fiction writers by depicting his male characters as extremely powerful. His woman characters are comparatively weak and meek. They either live up to the expectation of the archetypal male characters like Chhabi in Matimatal or Rabi, the hero, or they are an exploited lot in the flesh market of male dominated society.

Further Nandini explains,[14] Fakirmohan Senapati (1843-1918) is considered a pioneer in the field of Odia fiction. His "Rebati" published in 1898 is the first modern Odia short story. Much before social realism became the dominant mode in other literatures of the country, he had shown the way in the portrayal of life in the villages. His Chha Mana Atha Guntha is acclaimed as a modern classic. His other novels are Lachama, Mamu and Prayaschita. Fakir Mohan Senapati's women are truly renaissance women. Being a male writer, Fakirmohan Senapati understands the cause of women much better than most writers. The Indian woman is the victim of a terrible conflicting transitional period, torn between two different value systems. In spite of the status of equality bestowed upon her by law, it is difficult for her to change herself in the core and, for the society to free her of the age-old sanskar. Rebati is a teen age girl of the early part of the nineteenth century who has the quest for knowledge; she has a true renaissance spirit. She is encouraged by her father, mother and teacher Vasu with whom she has a platonic bond of the soul. But as it goes, her grandmother is very much against her education.

Sameer Master in the art of writing short stories stated that[15] he injected a new life in Odia literature in an environment of gloom and despair. His sence of humour remains unsurpassed in Odia literature. Discarding romantic themes, he wrote about the common man and his problems. Senapati could rightly be compared with the 20th Century great novelist like Premchand and Bibhutibhusan Banerjee. Even though he had no formal education, he proved to be an enlightened teacher, painter and a great administrator. In his writings, Odia Nationalism was the dominant theme. As a recognised man of literature, Senapati has made his place secure as a great prose writer in Odia.

Mohapatra stated that[16] Fakir Mohan Senapati (14 January 1843 - 14 June 1918) was an Indian writer in the Odia language, and is called the "Father of Modern Odia Literature. He is considered the Vyasakabi or founder figure of modern Odia literature. Fakir Mohan was born and brought up in the coastal town of Balasore. He grew up to be an administrator in ex-feudatory states. Enraged by the attempts of the Bengalis to marginalize and even, replace the Odia language by Bengali, he took to creative writing rather late. Though he had translated from Sanskrit, wrote poetry, and attempted many forms of literature, he is now known primarily as the father of modern Odia prose fiction. If either Fakir Mohan or his progeny had preserved his short story, "Lachmania" which he had written in the late 1860s, and which was published in the journal Bodhadayini, edited by himself in Balasore, Fakirmohan would certainly have been credited with having pioneered the genre in India. But as ill-luck would have it, except for a bare mention in his autobiography, the story cannot be traced, and thus his "Rebati" (1898) is widely recognized as the first Odia short story. "Rebati" is the story of a young innocent girl whose desire for education is placed in the context of a conservative Odia society, which is hit by the killer epidemic cholera. His other stories are "Patent Medicine"., "Dak Munshi","Adharma Bitta" etc.Other than short stories ,Fakir Mohan Senapati is also known for his novel Chha Maana Atha Guntha. It is the first Indian novel to deal with the exploitations of landless peasants by the feudal Lord. It was written much before the October revolution of Russia or much before the emerging of Marxist ideas in India.

Pratibha Roy, stated in her book that [17] "Balasore,the land of Fakir Mohan Senapati is the nursery of Odia literature", while paying tribute to the legendary personality on his 167th birth anniversary. Addressing a galaxy of intellectuals at an observance meeting, she expressed her views on the acclaimed novelist of modern Odia prose-fiction the uncrowned monarch of the Odia language movement. "Fakir Mohan's autobiography Atma Jiban Charita is not only the first of its kind in Odia, but remains the best and the most interesting in Indian languages," she said. With varied intellectual pursuits Vyasa Kabi was a successful poet, a pioneer novelist, short-story writer, an essayist, a translator, a critic, a satirist, an ardent social reformer par excellence, a capable administrator, a premier publisher and printer, an editor, a journalist of an un-paralleled spirit, observed other speakers . District collector Dr Alekh Padhiary said that the doyen of Odia literature experienced severe distress during his childhood when he got not much support in his fight for his language under threat of survival. However, he relentlessly and single-handedly fought for the survival of Odia language and claimed a special status in the mainstream of national linguistic order. Dr. Padhiary pointed out, "He will reign the heart and soul of every Odia as long as the language and literature will exist on earth".

Jagadish reveals that[18] not only with the themes of women education, womens rightful place in society the story "Rebati" has also influenced a lot of short story writers of Odisha in later period .In early Eighties of last century Jagadish Mohanty, wrote a story based on the protagonist character "Rebati" and it made a new tradition .Since then hundreds of stories have been written on the women's agony ,where "Rebati" represents the women's fate in changing scenario of time. Asit Kumar Mohanty later edited all the stories, along with both Fakir Mohan and Jagadish's "Rebati" in two of his collections under the same title.

Asit Kumar stated in his book that[19] from Rebati of Fakir Mohan to Sarojini Sahoo , the cultural scenario of Odisha has changed a lot. In 1871 for the first time a school for Hindu girls was set-up at Cuttack in the house of Abhinash Chandra Chattopadhaya. Even after the school ran for 10 years at Cuttack city, only four Hindu girls could be enrolled. The role of Fakir Mohan Senapati, Sudhal Dev, the Raja of Bamanda and T.E Ravenshaw, then Commissioner of Cuttack (Odisha) was significant. Among the women personalities, the efforts of Reba Roy and Rani of Khallikote in spreading female education in the beginning of the 20th century were indeed heartening. The most laudable effort was the Utkal Mahila Conference held in Berhampur in 1924 . Gandhiji's visit to Odisha for the first time in 1921 obviously had its effect. Smt Rasamani Devi, Sarala Devi, Kuntala Kumari Sabat, Sarojini Choudhury took pioneering interest in establishing the Participation of many Odia women in the historic Karachi Congress session in 1931 which paved the way for greater role in national movement. The spread of the Civil disobedience movement in Odisha was mostly due to the All Orissa Women's Council which had members from different parts of the state with Kuntala Kumari as its President. They declared the 5 rights of women over their body, over the possessions of their husbands, over their own husband and children and over their religion. Women like Rama Devi, Malati Devi, Annapurna Devi,Godavari Devi worked for the socio economic upliftment of Odia women, especially the rural women. After the independence women such as Shubhadra Mahtab, Malati Devi, Rama Devi, Sarala Devi, Satyavati Devi continued to work for social transformation. In later period, the entry of Nandini Satpathy who hailed from a political background and had been a student activist and who rose to be the Chief

Minister of the State turned the scenario, totally different from that of 1898 , when Fakir Mohan had written the story “Rebati”. In literary field, the women participation was not remarkable up to seventies of the last Century, Kuntala Kumari Sabat, Bidyut Prabha Devi, Binapani Mohanty and Nandini Satpathy were a few names can be worth mentioning. After Seventies, some female writers like Sarojini Sahoo , Jayanti Ratha, Susmita Bagchi.Yashodhara Mishra, Hiranmayee Mishra, Chirashree IndraSingh, Gayatri Saraf., Mamata Choudhury emerged, among whom Sarojini Sahoo played a significant role for her feministic approach in fiction.

In an international conference titled "The Literary View from Below", held in Delhi (January 3-5, 2007) organised by the DCRC, Delhi University, “Fakir Mohan Senapati ” Project, USA and the South Asian Program, Cornell University, the three perspectives to bear on Fakir Mohan Senapati's Odia novel “Chha Mana Atha Guntha” (Six Acres and a Third) were highlighted. The two panel discussions that flanked the conference addressed the central question of language in Indian literature. The panelists on Fakir Mohan’s novels Namwar Singh, Harish Trivedi, Manoranjan Mohanty, G.K. Das and Chaman Lal (Delhi), Amiya Dev (Kolkata), V. Narayan Rao and Satya P. Mohanty (U.S.) argued on a very significantly intelligent play on languages. Namwar Singh resisted the Bakhtinian implications of this thesis. All agreed that the novel could be read as a cautionary account of the process whereby a rich heteroglossia was giving way to an impoverished monolingualism, designated by the nationalist shift to the concept of the mother tongue.

RajKumar explains in his book that[20] Fakir Mohan Senapati’s novel “Chha Mana Atha Guntha” (Six Acres and a Third) set in colonial Indian society during the early decades of the19th century tells a tale of wealth and greed, of property and theft. On one level, it is the story of an evil landlord, Ramachandra Mangaraj, who exploits poor peasants and uses the new legal system to appropriate the property of others. But this is merely one of the themes of the novel; as the text unfolds, it reveals several layers of meaning and implications. Toward the end of Mangaraj's story, he is punished by the law and we hear how the "Judge Sahib" ordered that his landed estate, his "zamindari," be taken away. It is sold to a lawyer, who — as rumour in the village has it — "will come with ten palanquins followed by five horses and two hundred foot-soldiers" to take possession of Mangaraj's large estate. The ordinary villagers react to this news by reminding one another of an old saying: "O horse, what difference does it make to you if you are stolen by a thief? You do not get much to eat here; you will not get much to eat there. No matter who becomes the next master, we will remain his slaves. We must look after our own interests." Fakir Mohan Senapati's novel is written from the perspective of the horse, the ordinary villager, and the foot-soldier — in other words, the labouring poor of the world. Although it contains a critique of British colonial rule, the novel offers a powerful indictment of many other forms of social and political authority as well. What makes Six Acres unusual is that its critical vision is embodied in its narrative style and in the complex way it is organized as a literary text. Senapati's novel (the Odia original was serialized in 1897-1899 and published as a book in 1902) is justly seen as representing the apex of the tradition of literary realism in 19th century Indian literature. But its realism is complex and sophisticated, not simply mimetic; the novel seeks to analyze and explain social reality instead of merely holding up a mirror to it. The linguistic innovations of Six Acres and a Third, need to be appreciated in this wider context. These innovations changed Odia literature forever, and inaugurated the age of modern Odia prose, which have been based on a vision of social equality and cultural self-determination. Senapati was no romantic nationalist, and his conception of language was based on his progressive social vision. In his prose works, he sought to popularize an egalitarian literary medium that was sensitive enough to draw on the rich idioms of ordinary Odia, the language of the paddy fields and the village markets. If he saw the imposition of other languages like Persian, English, or Bengali on Odia as a form of linguistic colonialism, it is because he considered the interests of Odia — much like the interests of any linguistic community — to be tied to democratic cultural and social access to power.

Prabhakar stated that[21] by reading a novel by George Eliot alongside a novel by her Indian contemporary Fakir Mohan Senapati, this essay offers a cross-cultural comparison of fictional realisms. In *The Mill on the Floss* (1860), Eliot used a learned narrator and extended forms of free indirect discourse to examine humble life with unprecedented sympathy and complexity, but the formal dissonance between the authoritative narrative voice and class-marked forms of represented speech construct a view of the lower classes from "above"—that is, from the vantage point of the educated middle-class readers whom Eliot implicitly constructs as the agents of history. By contrast, Senapati's *Six Acres and a Third* (1897–99), written in the demotic Indian language of Odia, achieves a view from "below" through an ironic narrator who parodies the very type of learned discourse that Eliot (at the opposite end of the British empire) deploys as the instrument of liberal humanism. By evacuating a discursive cultural authority, Senapati produces a dialogic interplay of voices that brings the reader into the lives of his impoverished villagers without sentimentality or condescension—an achievement that in some ways resembles later European modernism as much as the realism of Eliot.

Mansingh stated that[22] the regretful confession of his misdeeds in his new Dewani life, as a part and parcel of administrative endeavour proved his extraordinarily natural purity of his personality and generosity. An aspirant reformer, innovator, Fakir Mohan always reminded us of the German literary creator Goethe, as a dewan of Wymer, a small German feudal state. Had Fakir Mohan spent his administrative life time like Goethe in one state, we would have seen an established ideal state under his guidance.

Brajamohan explain that,[23] Fakir Mohan began his career as the builder of Odisha's modern literary edifice. The contribution of Fakir

Mohan to Odia literature during the renaissance of Odia literature is great. He fought most of his life for the cause of the Odia language like a general in the battlefield. Fakir Mohans's life can be termed as a renowned history of defence and self-manifestation of Odia literature. Fakir Mohan Senapati, not usually named as the father of modern Oriya literature distinguished himself as a short story writer, novelist, poet, translator and essayist.

Prafulla Chandra stated that[24] the announcement of new education policy was a challenge to Bengali's supremacy in Odisha. In a meeting at Cuttack Debating Society. Rajendralal Mitra pointed out the difficulties of the printing of Odia books and it also hampered the progress of Odisha. In Balasore, Kanti Chandra Bhattacharya wrote a book "Odiya Swatantra Bhasa Nae". All of a sudden Fakir Mohan mobilized public opinion through organizing meetings, Public speeches, writing in Sambad Bahika. A committee was formed by him and some of his friends to save the odia language.

Surendra explain in his book that[25] Fakir Mohan began writing short stories at the middle age from a life experience of great agonies and sufferings. So the stories bear the evidence of intimate knowledge of human psychology and vivid expression. There are reformative ideas in education and culture in the stories. So not only from the literary point of view, but also from the social consideration , these stories are very much precious.

Surendra narrated that[26] Fakir Mohan wrote four novels. Namely Chhamana Athaguntha, Lachhama, Mamu and Prayaschitta. All these novels were written in the last phase of Fakir Mohan's life. Besides these, Fakir Mohan in a letter to Biswanath Kar, mentioned about the writing of a long story "Bisamanji' on the request of Nandakishore, He wrote it and later change the same story into a novel.

Brajamohan explains that[27] the publication of Chhaman Athaguntha was a memorable event in the history of novels. Before Fakir Mohan, perhaps no such cruel picture of exploitation and plunder was published in a heart touching manner in any Indian language and literature. When the novel was published periodically in 'Utkal Sahitya", it made much fuss in the reader's society. The period of writing of 'Chhamana Athaguntha' was from October 1897 to 1899 and the event of its description was from 1801 to 1840. In this novel He has started a discussion on the relation between the rich and the downtrodden class before 1900. But Bankim Chandra and Sarat Chandra of Bengali literature and Prem Chand of Hindi literature started their efforts after 1900. So Fakir Mohan could be regarded as epoch-making writer among all bringing a revolutionary change to Indian literature.

Again Brajamohan explains that[28] the last novel of Fakir Mohan was 'Prayaschita' which describes how the tradition-bound society was destroyed with the contact of western civilization. He was not a man belonging to the age of 'Lachhma' or Chhaman Athaguntha' but he belonged to the contemporary age of 'Mamu' and 'Prayhschitta'. That is why it is said that Fakir Mohan has depicted a partial picture of his family life in the novel 'Prayaschitta'.

Brajamohan narrated that[29] for the first time Fakir Mohan gave life to common speech forms. The spoken language of the common man was the language of Fakir Mohan's prose. Before him only Sarala Das and Jagannath Das had shown their ability for unprecedented creativity in language of Odia literature. At last in the world of Odia prose, no other writer except Fakir Mohan had this qualification. In a true sense, he was an unrivalled emperor in prose style of Odia literature. When Odia literature was ignored and undeveloped, Fakir Mohan made his appearance. Had Fakir Mohan not been born at that crucial moment, the Odia prose literature would have lagged fifty years behind.

Mohanty explains in his book that[30] besides Indian stories and characters he also took the stories and characters from foreign countries. His subjects included Josephine, Cleopatra: the Rape of Lucrece and Russo Japanese War of 1905. Radhanath Roy, Madhusudan Rao friend of Fakir

Mohan had not dared to go outside Odisha and India. But Fakir Mohan's literary works ranged beyond the frontiers. His poetic creations like 'Utkal Krusaka' 'Utkal Bhumi' , 'Utkal Yubaka' were the products of his deep involvement in the Odia nationalistic ideas and inspired thousands of his fellowmen with his message.

Surendra narrated that[31] Fakir Mohan was very much interested in the development of Sanskrit literature. During his first service as Dewan in Nilgiri, he established first Sanskrit tolls for the Brahamin students. His ambition was the rise and development of Sanskrit literature in India.

Prafulla narrated that[32] there was a two hundred year's history of Odisha behind the creation of Fakir Mohan's literature. According to N. Samantray, the four novels of Fakir Mohan depicted the history of two hundred years in Odia social life. In the opinion of Mayadhar Mansingh, behind the great literary success of Fakir Mohan's novels there stood the two hundred years of socio-political history of the Odia race. In the language of Gopal Chandra Mishra, the subject matter of Fakir Mohan's short stories and novels are excerpted from Odia society and history and it is well-imagined in a planned way and in an adept linguistic style of the two hundred years of society and the contemporary social surroundings. The periodicity of his novels is as follows:

Chhaman Atagunta --1897- 1899 (Utkal Sahitya Patrika & as a Novel in 1902)

Lachhama -1903

Mamu – 1913

Prayaschitta - 1915

Again Prafulla explains that[33] the subtle implications in the aftermath of the downfall of feudal powers and disturbance in land settlement in the beginning of the British rule are the historical events described in Chhaman Athaguntha. It ruined the village economy based on village units resulting in a very unjust and cruel way of the British rule. Bengali Officials, Police, Kutchery officials and the new zamindar class deprived the Odias of all sorts of freedom and social rights. Chhaman Athaguntha is eternal example of exploitation.

As a writer, Fakir Mohan Senapati has contributed a lot to Odia literature. He is solely responsible for bringing Odia literature alive, which has now gained immense popularity among the people. His novels reflect the socio-political aspects of the state during the eighteenth and the nineteenth century. Some of his well-known novels are- Chhamana Athaguntha, Lachhama, Mamu and Prayaschita. Another book titled Atma Jeevan Charita is considered to be the first autobiography in Odia language and literature. Chhamana Athaguntha was first serialized during the last decade of the nineteenth century and was published as a book in 1902.

REFERENCES

1. C. R. Kothari, Research Methodology, method and techniques, New Delhi, wiley eastern limited, 1985, p.35.

2. C. D. Govindrao, English Novelists and Education, Ph.D, English Mysore University, 1955, quoted by M.B.Buch (ed) in A survey of research in education, Borada: CASE, 1974, pp. 36-37.

3. S. M. Divekar, A critical study of the educational philosophy of Upanishads, Ph.D. Education, 1960, quoted by M. B. Buch (ed) op. cit. pp. 33-34.

4. M. C. Charlu, The educational philosophy of Bhagvat Gita, Ph.D. Education, Sardar Patel University, 1971, quoted by M. B. Buch (ed) op. cit.p.30.

5. D. C. Jha, An analytical study of educational principle in Kamayani, Ph.D, Education, Bihar University, 1973, quoted by M. B. Buch (ed)in second survey of research in education.(1972-1978), Baroda, society for educational research and development, 1979,p.33.

6. N.Sharma, Essential of education in the Jain literature, Ph. D Education, Patna University, 1976, quoted by M. B. Buch (ed) op.cit, 1979,p.36.

7. M. Venkateswarlu, The educational philosophy as reflected in the Mohabharat, Ph. D, Education, Andhra University, 1978, quoted by M. B. Buch (ed) op.cit, 1986, p.55.

8. M. Dubey, Educational philosophy of Upanishad, Ph.D, Education, Sampurnand Sanskrit university, 1980, quoted by M.B.Buch (ed) op.cit, 1986, pp. 39-40.

9. C. Biswal,A study of the contribution of Radhanath Rai and Madhusudan Rao in the 19th century educational situation in Orissa, Ph.D, Education, Sambalpur University, 1989.

10. R. G. Prabhune, A critical study of the literature of sane Guruji from the educational point of view, Ph.D. Education, Sivaji University, 1990, quoted in fifth survey of educational research (1988-1992), Vol. II, New Delhi :NCERT,2000,pp.804-805.

11. S.S.Lohakare, A study of the educational philosophy in Samartha Ramdas Swamy's Dasbodha with reference to the values of life, Ph.D, Education Nagpur University, 1991, quoted in fifth survey of educational research (1988-1992), Vol.II, New Delhi :NCERT,2000,pp.800.

12. J.V.Boulton, Fakir Mohan Senapati, His life and prose fiction, Bhubaneswar, Orissa Sahitya Academy, 1993.

13. Sahu, Nandini – The position of women in Oriya literature

14. Ibid,pp.23-24

15. Ranjan, Sameer. 1999. Uihunka Palatijauthiba Manishamane (Man turns to an Anthill: A Collection of Oriya Short stories). Puri: Biswamitra Publications.

16. Mohapatra, Prabhu Kalyan (April 2005) "Fakir Mohan : Father of Modern Oriya Literature" "Orissa Review-April-2005" p.61

17. Roy,Pratibha, Indian Literature, Vol. 172, 1996, P- 73.

18. Album"-Short Stories Collection Jagadish Mohanty, Publishrd by Grantha Mandir, Binode Behari ,Cuttack

19. Rebati"-Edited by Asit Kumar Mohanty and published by Friends Publishers, Binode Behati, Cuttack

20. Kumar, Raj. People at the bottom: The untouchables in Indian novels. In The Fourth World: Journal of the Marginalised People, No. 8, Oct. 1998. Bhubaneswar: NISWASS.
21. Palaka, Prabhakar. 2001. The voice of the oppressed: Translation of Sameer Ranjan's Uihunka Palatijauthiba Manishamane. A Collection of Oriya Short Stories into English, Unpublished M. Phil dissertation, JNU, New Delhi.
22. Mansingh, Mayadhar, Saraswati Fakir Mohan (Oriya), 1981, Cuttack. PP.91-92.
23. Mohanty, Brajamohan, Adhunika Oriya Sahitya (Oriya),1963, Cuttack,P.50.
24. Mohanty, Prafulla Chandra, (ed), Senapati Sahityaloka (Oriya), 1989, Balasore, P.21.
25. Mohanty, Surendra, Fakir Mohan Samikshya (Oriya), 1972, cuttack, PP.161-163
26. Mohanty, Surendra, op.cit.P. 233.
27. Mohanty, Brajamohan, Oriya Sahitya Adhunika Juga, Part-I (Oriya), 1966, Cuttack, PP.90-91.
28. Ibid.P.106.
29. Mohanty, Brajamohan, Oriya Sahitya Adhunika Juga, Part-I (Oriya), 1966, Cuttack, P.105.
30. Mohanty, N, Oriya Nationalism: Quest for a United Orissa, 1982, New Delhi, P.73.
31. Mohanty, Surendra, Fakir Mohan Samikshya (Oriya), 1972, Cuttack, P.12.
32. Mohanty, Prafulla Chandra, op. cit, P.32.
33. Ibid., P.173.

♦♦♦

CHAPTER-III

ODISHA DURING THE TIME OF FAKIR MOHAN SENAPATI

CHAPTER III

ODISHA DURING THE TIME OF FAKIR MOHAN SENAPATI

Odisha of Fakir Mohan Senapati's time (1843-1918) was politically dismembered, socially unconscious and exploited, economically crippled, yet culturally envisioned and educationally ignored. 'From 1803 to 1936, the Odia people lay dispersed in the presidencies of Bengal and Madras, the Central provinces and the twenty four feudatory states. Odisha was constituted as a separate state on the 1st of April, 1936. The process of amalgamating all the feudatory states was completed on 1st January, 1949 when the state of Odisha assumed its present territorial identity.[1] During the time of Fakir Mohan Senapati Odisha was, in fact, passing through a critical phase. It was subject to instrumental changes in different field of development. A brief account of the changes in its physical features, political scenario, social system, economic condition, cultural background and public instruction is presented in the following paragraphs.

British occupation of the coastal districts of Odisha was almost forty years old by the time Fakir Mohan was born on January 13, 1843, in Balasore, one of the coastal districts. The political condition of Odisha at the time of British occupation was extremely unstable. For long, Odisha was a hotbed of conflict between different Muslim rulers on the one hand and the indigenous power elite on the other. Immediately before the British occupation Odisha had come under the hegemony of a Maratha chieftain ruling from Nagpur. Since Marathas were not interested in establishing a State or the rule of the law, they used the area only for extortion. The British East India Company took advantage of this fluid political condition in order to occupy the area quite easily. The British justified their imperialism in the name of establishing the rule of law and providing "order" in a "failed state." They also constructed a befitting historiography which claimed that only fifty East India Company soldiers marched into the Barabati Fort (the seat of power of these districts) and established the company rule without almost any resistance from local militia. But, the so-called rule of law or order was so elusive and the economic exploitation so harsh that there were popular uprisings against the British occupation within months. However, it took almost a decade for these uprisings to consolidate into a major revolt in the form of the Paika Rebellion of 1817. Although the colonial administration and historiography has tried to designate this as an insurgency mounted by the remnants of the traditional feudal class, it was actually a mass movement involving people from all sections of Odia society. The revolt was inevitably mauled by the company forces armed with superior weapons. The local militia lacked training badly and was using very archaic weapons.

The quelling of the revolt demoralized the Odia community completely, even as it somewhat tempered the British maraudery. The company subsequently made some constructive gestures and tried to establish a semblance of rule of law, but this was done in order to further its own imperialistic designs. It ushered in institutions of 'modernisation' like the school, the judiciary and land reforms. Under its aegis the missionaries of various Christian denominations established schools, health-care system, and printing presses to start publication of books in the vernacular language of Odia. However, many Odias could not participate in the 'civilising mission' of the British at that time because of their lack of will, economic impoverishment, and state of demoralisation. The inaction of Odias at a time when imperialism was bringing about massive changes in social structures both by its coercive and ideological state apparatus created a vacuum in the social space. In the meantime, due to their early exposure to the British administration and the forces of "modernisation" which it unleashed, the neighboring Bengalis had consolidated themselves into a sizable comprador class. The British had become increasingly dependent on this comprador class for the smooth functioning of the administration. This Bengali comprador class started manning most of the government jobs in Odisha. They spread their sub colonizing tentacles by appropriating the Zamindari estates in Odisha, especially after the promulgation of the Sunset Law. In order to perpetuate their hold over property, jobs, and hence, access to power, the Bengali elite wanted to valorize the Bengali language and marginalise the local language Odia. Writing about the sorry state of the Odias at that time, Natabara Samantaray cites the following opinion of Mr. Nolan, the Collector of Cuttack in 1879: "It may be doubted whether the Odia is holding his own in the struggle for existence. The Bengali is ousting him from the land and from service; the Bengali, the Marwaris and the Europeans, from trade; the Telugu from the rougher kinds of labour".

3.1 PHYSICAL FEATURES

Odisha of Fakir Mohan Senapati's time was a cultural unit without a definite political boundary. It was a name usually given to the geographical area in which the Odia-speaking people occupied a dominant place. 'The Odias were administered by five separate political authorities. : (i) Bengal and its Odisha division. (ii) Chhotanagpur, (iii) The Central Provinces, (iv) Madras and (v) the feudatory states of Odisha'.[2]

The boundaries of Odisha underwent changes from time to time. In the 19th century, it was reduced to the Odisha division of Bengal presidency and the twenty four feudatory states. The Odisha division included the districts of Cuttack, Puri, Balasore and Angul-Kondhmal, and its boundaries stretched form Bengal in the north to Madras Presidency in the sought and from Chhotnagpur plateau in the west to the Bay of Bengal in the east. It lies between 19^0 28' and 28^0 04N Latitude and 82^0 38' and $87^{0.}$31' longitude. Sambalpur district was a part of Orissa division upto 1861. It was taken away and merged with the Central Provinces for a period of 44 years and was again amalgamated in Odisha division in 1905. The twenty four feudatory states formed part and parcel of Odisha both from cultural and linguistic view point though the British did not directly administer them. The commissioner of Odisha was the ex-officio Superintendent of these states and also exercised the power of session's judge and High Court in respect of them. The total area of Odisha division was 9.919 British square miles whereas the twenty four feudatory states had an area of 28.046 British square miles. According to 1901 census. The population of Orissa division and the feudatory states was reported to be 43, 43,150 and 31, 73,395 respectively. [3]

The present day Odisha extends from $17^0 49'$ N to $22^0 34'$ N latitude and from $81^0 29'$ to $87^0 29'$ E longitude on the eastern coast of India. It has an area of about 1,55,707 square kilometers according to the census of India 1981. Its is bounded by the states of West Bengal in the north-east, Bihar in the north. Chhatisgarh in the west. Andhra Pradesh in the south and the Bay of Bengal in the east.[4]

So far as the geographical condition of Odisha during the time of Fakir Mohan Senapati was concerned, it was a heterogeneous area. It encompassed two geographical regions. Namely,the coastal plains comprising of the districts of Cuttack. Puri, Balasore and the plain areas of Ganjam district, and the highlands constituted of rugged hills, uninhabited jungles. And deep water courses surrounded by pathless wildernesses of forestes, valleys, and pervaded by pestilential atmosphere.[5] Almost all the feudatory states like Ganjam malia Goomsur, Angul, Kondhmal and Sambalpur were located in these highlands. About one third of the whole area of Odisha remained wild and inaccessible because of the hill and forest.[6]

The important rivers flowing through Odisha, like the Mahanadi, the Brahmani, the Baitarini, the Budhabalanga, the Salandi, the Rushikulya, the Bhargabi, the Indravati, the Subarnarekha, the Kathajori, the Kuakhai etc. greatly affected the socio-economic life of the people. These treacherous rivers caused frequent divesting floods and also created communication problems.[7]

Like geography, environment is also a vital feature. The climatic condition in Odisha was found both moderate as well as extreme. It was moderate in the plain but extreme in the highlands featured by hills and forests. The repeated and sudden change in temperature was another characteristic of the climatic condition of Odisha. The natural calamities like floods, droughts, cyclones and famines were interrelated to climate. Again the barren and unproductive soils, absence of communication facilities like roads, and the simple conservative, ignorant and wild nature of the people were some indispensable ingredients of the physical design of Odisha.[8]

Thus the physical features of Odisha during the time of Fakir Mohan Senapati were characterized by the changing-territorial boundaries, odd geography, frequent natural calamities, varied climatic conditions, lack of communications and above all its simple but ignorant and backward inhabitants.

3.2 POLITICAL SCENARIO

Fakir Mohan's first novel, *Six Acres and a Third*, records the political and economic situation immediately after the occupation of the coastal districts of Odisha by the British East India Company. It highlights the consequences of the greed of the British rulers and their attempt to impose an alien economic and land revenue system. On the one hand the British saved the common people from the violence and extortion of Maratha Marauders, but, on the other, they ruined the traditional society in such a manner that the common people were disinherited from all their traditional occupations and professions. They were tied down to just one profession, i.e., agriculture. Soon, they were even disinherited from their lands by the Bengali sub-*colonisers* and were reduced to the status of farmhands. While the people in common were losing the moorings in their own land, a new privileged class was getting consolidated. This new feudal class consisted of the Bengali officers of the Company, the landlords from Bengal and the few manipulative Odias who used their access to British education and their proximity to power to rise economically and socially. This neo-feudal were aping their colonial masters and were much more oppressive towards the common people, at whose cost they had risen socially. Fakirmohan's third novel, *Mamu*, dramatizes this scenario of the latter half of the colonial rule. The last novel, *Prayaschita*, maps the breakdown of the traditional social fabric and cultural norms under the impact of the grafting of colonialism. It demonstrates the process of commodification of education, fragmentation of family and rigidification of caste divide due to various British administrative policies and alien cultural habits. We will try to analyse the process by looking at his most popular novel *Six Acres and a Third.*

During the time of Fakir Mohan Senapati Odisha was placed under several administrative jurisdictions under the British administration at the helm of affair. As a result the Odia- speaking people suffered from the injustice of political dismemberment for nearly a century, and were exploited culturally, politically and economically. They formed a minority in all the administrative jurisdictions and this very fact threatened the sanctity of their language and culture.

The disastrous Na Anka famine of 1866 resulted in a new era of consciousness in Odisha. In the last part of nineteenth century, the progress in the field of education, communication, trade and commerce and the growth of vernacular press led to political awareness of the Odia-speaking people. A section of literate Odias tried to analyze the emerging problems coming in the way of an independent Odia State. They expressed their feeling in the form of an odia movement demanding amalgamation of Odia-speaking tracts lying under different administrations. In 1876, Raja Baikunthanath De of Balasore and Bichitrananda Pattnaik and memorialized to the Government for union under a single administration of all the scattered Oriya tracts.[9] Mr. Cooke, the then commissioner of Odisha, supporting the union of all Oriya-speaking tracts, wrote in the administrative report of Orissa division, published in the Calcutta Gazette supplement dated 23rd October 1895.

As a question of administrative reform for which there is much to be said, I have to advocate the extension of the divisional boundaries so as to mauled the whole area populated by races speaking the Odia-languages or at any rate, some definite areas adjoining Orissa where the Odia language prevails. Odisha is a very small division, both in area and population, and there is no doubt that the commissioner could find time to deal with a very material addition to his work. The areas that I refer to are the Sambalpur district of the Chhatisgarh division of the Central provinces with the tributary states of Patna, Sonepur, Rairakhol, Bamra, Kalahandi, the whole or part of the Ganjam district with the states of kimidi and Ghumsur. Among the reasons for this change are, as I have said, the uniting in a single division and placing under the same laws and rules the whole local population, instead of having a portion of it forming insignificant item of the Central Provinces and another portion forming an equally insignificant item of the Madras presidency. I am in possession of a map of India, dated 1841, in which, either or ethnological or political grounds, the province of Odisha includes the two portions of territory that I have proposed to absorb in this division.[10]

On 30.12.1903, the Indian National Congress in its XIX session passed the resolution on the subject of territorial dismemberment which contributed significantly to the Odia movement.[11] The Odia movement gained further momentum under the aegis of Utkal Sammelan (Utkal union conference) - the fifth political association of Odisha; established in 1903 by Madhusudan Das and a group of English educated Odias with the support of the leading feudatory chiefs of Odisha.

Though Sambalpur and five feudatory states were transferred from the central provinces to the Odisha division in 1905, Ganjam area still remained a part of the Madras Presidency. It could not be transferred to Odisha division due to stiff opposition of the Madras Government. This non-excision of Ganjam from Madras destroyed the hopes of Odias irredentists for a political union and gave to vigorous agitation under the stewardship of the Utkal union conference.[12] However, the political status of Odisha division remained unchanged till 1912 when the province of Bihar and Odisha was created.[13] Justifying the creation of the province of Bihar and Odisha, the Viceroy 'Lord Hardinge' mentioned:

The Odias like the Biharees have little in common with Bengalis and we propose to leave Odisha with Bihar and Chhotnagpur. We believe that this arrangement will well accord with popular sentiment in Odisha.[14]

However the formation of the province of Bihar and Odisha failed to satisfy the Odias. It was mainly because of two reasons. Firstly they did not want to be tagged with Bihar, and second the non-inclusion of Ganjam area with the new provinces. For the elite community the creation of the new province was like a political earthquake'.[15] Reacting to the formation of the new Province, Lord Curzon as a member of the House of Lords, made a scathing remark.

This province of yours has been drawn up without the slightest regard to the interests or views of the inhabitants.[16]

However from 1912 to 1936 when the separate province of Odisha was created, the province of Bihar and Odisha provided ample opportunity to the Odias elites to have a trial of strength with the colonial government. It was the most formative period of political awareness in Odisha when one finds the Odia speaking people responding whole-heartedly to the call of Mahatma Gandhi. This period also witnessed the culmination of their search for an identity-the birth of linguistic province.[17]

Simultaneous with the movement for its territorial unity. Odisha marched on the path of freedom struggle with the rest of India. The Bengal extremists with active assistance of Odia inhabitants worked for anti-government activities in a daring spirit.[18] Actually the Odias had already started developing anti-British feeling even before the great revolt of 1857. This movement in Odisha was led by Veer Surendra Sai of Sambalpur. The great revolt of 1857 had been suppressed elsewhere in India by 1858.

The political leaders of Odisha were divided into two groups. The first group followed the path of constitutional struggle set by Madhusudan Das to achieve the goal of amalgamation of scattered Odia-speaking tracts. The second was the Satyavadi group of scholar-politicans led by Gopabandhu Das devoted itself wholeheartedly to the cause of national freedom. The public opinion and the press in Odisha got influenced by these two treads in the 1920. The Samaj, a weekly Odia newspaper established by Gopabandhu Das in 1919 promoted the cause of nationalism as never before. Boycott of schools, colleges, Government institutions, courts, and demonstrations were organized daily at Cuttack, Puri, Balasore and Sambalpur.[19] As a response to the call of non-cooperation given by Mahatma Gandhi, the nationalist leaders of Odisha encouraged the people to observe everything relating to the British Government, including the government school. As a result many students left Government schools. And to provide educational facilities to those students some National Schools were established by congress leaders in Odisha. One such school was also established at Sambalpur.[20]

It was unique response to Mahatma Gandhi's call from all sections of people when he toured Odisha in March 1921. Further the visit of other national leaders like Rajgopalchari, Motlal Neheru and Subash Chandra Boss among others. In 1922 gave a fillip to the national movement in Odisha.[21] The movement went to the grassroot when under Kastaram Ganda the depressed classes came forward to court arrest and to suffer imprisonment. A special feature of the Odisha non-cooperation movement was that at some places like Kanika, the movement took the form of agrarian uprising of the most downtrodden peasantry.[22]

The Odia member in the provincial legislature, and the legislative assembly of India played a very significant role in the political development of Odisha during the decade following the non-cooperation movement. However the death of Gopabandhu Das a leader of integrity and great organizing ability, in 1928 administered a rude shock to the struggle for freedom in Odisha.[23]

While the freedom struggle took its full course in the British administered Odisha under the leadership of National Congress, spontaneous popular movements became a distinctive feature of the Gadjat areas where the people rose both against feudal tyranny of the princely rulers and their overlord, the britishers. It was the early efforts of the Odia luminaries like Madhusadan Das, Gopabandhu Das, Gangadhar Meher, Fakir Mohan Senapati. Fakir Mohan Senapati and others, which enable Odisha to emerge as independent state on 1st April 1936 followed by the independence of India on 15th August 1947.[24]

Through Odisha of Fakir Mohan Senapati's time was politically dismembered, it was also the most formative period in the political history of Odisha. The period was marked by the growth of political awareness and unity among the Odia speaking People. Fakir Mohan Senapati had a close – rapport with political leadership and minutely observed the political activities of the time. Through his literary activities and personal contacts. Fakir Mohan Senapati influenced the political happening of his time.

3.3 SOCIAL SYSTEM

Odishan society of Fakir Mohan Senapati's time consisted of two major groups the caste Hindus residing in the plains and the tribal staying in the wild and inaccessible highlands. The people in general were simple, conservative, superstitious and dogmatic. The psyche of the people was dominated by various myths, magic. witchcraft, sorcery and sacrifices.[25] This subjected the then society to be the victim of three infamous and gruesome social practices. One was sati[26] which prevailed among the high caste Hindus of the plains and the other two were human sacrifices called meriah.[27] and infanticide which were found among the tribals.[28]

Fakir Mohan's representation of colonial reality and its critique is rooted in his engagement with a sense of history and a peculiar notion of time. Traditional Indian thought held a cyclic view of time in which history is a terrestrial reworking of a metaphysical Fate. Of course fate is mentioned quite often in Fakir Mohan's works (including *Six Acres*), but unlike traditional Indian notions of fate, it does not transcend the social reality and the historical process.

Fakir Mohan's notions of history as a process and time as progression could have been imbibed from the Western episteme. It is fruitful to remember here that Fakir Mohan started his career as a literatteur with the translation of Ishwarchandra Vidyasagar's Bengali text *Jivan Carita* and a history text book for schools entitled *Bharatbarshar Itihas* Vol. I&II. The *Jivan Carita*, in fact, was a collection of short biographical sketches of a few major western scientists. The translation and the text book are indicators of the fact that although Fakir Mohan ideologically was a staunch opponent of colonialism and its knowledge systems he admired the radical possibilities he saw in Western Science and in Renaissance humanism. In many of his writings, he celebrates modern modes of communication and the general mobility of individuals and civilisations. His peculiar notion of time, too, could have been the result of his attempt to synthesis Indian notions of fate with Western notions of time as a linear progression. On the one hand, Fakir Mohan sees the progression of time as irreversible, and on the other, time is seen as the unfolding of a divine will. The contradiction tempers his world view so that he sees colonialism both as fate accompli and as part of a process which can be shaped by conscious social action.

The Odias as a nation had social manners and customs peculiar to themselves. But due to forced contacts with alien races in the outlying tracts of Orissa, these had undergone slight changes in the 19th century. However the people of Odisha were different in nature from their counterparts in the adjacent provinces. For instance, the Odia Brahmin belonged to the gauda sect and was a non-vegetarian while his telugu counterpart belonged to the Dravidian sect and was a vegetarian. Again as regards marriage, the Telugu people married their own sister's daughters but this system was looked down upon by the Odisha.[29]

Like all other factors, religion played an important role in the social life of man in Odisha. According to O' Malley, the Hindus of Odisha as elsewhere were a most conservative, devoutly religious and priestridden people strictly observing ceremonial Purity.[30]

As regards marriage, the parents were more worried about their daughters than for their son's marriage. The marriageable age of a girl was much lower than that of the boy. The dowry evil was not so widespread nor so virulent or violent, as in the present day situation. Marriage within one's own sub-caste and of course within his caste only was approved by the society. Among the lower Hindu castes where the Brahmin priest did not officiate, the marriages were performed either by caste elders or by the caste headman or by some low caste priests.[31]

In the 19th century Odisha women were religious, tolerant, well dressed, modest and highly respected in the society. Mr. S.P.Rice, I.C.S., once collector of Ganjam, in his book Essays on Native South Indian Life, discussed regarding the subject of female modesty in Odisha. With the first hand knowledge of the conditions of Ganjam, Mr. Rice Wrote:

Odia women have high sense of modesty. It is not confined to the high class alone. Even the women whom the necessities of life drive to work in the fields are exceptionally modest and respectful. A coolie woman will turn her face away from you, and as you pass, she will draw her cloth more securely across her breast.[32]

The contemporary Odia litterateur Fakir Mohan Senapati reflected the misery of women in his literary works. His poem entitled Bidhabara Abhisapa (Curse of the widow) dealt with the cruelties inflicted on the widows.[33] Utkalamani Gopabandhu Das also highlighted the suffering of women in his poem Karakabita and in other literary creations as well.[34]

Child-marriage was another sort of social exploitation of Odia women during the time. Referring to their pitiable condition, A. Sutton remarked:

She (woman) is scarcely a girl before she is a wife, a mother and perhaps a widow. In Odisha she is often betrothed in mere infancy without any power of her own to choose or refuse, and before she enters her teens has been married and conducted to her husband's house for life.[35]

Odisha of Fakir Mohan Senapati's time was also marked by severe social exploitation and corruption. Exploitation of the poor villagers by the Zamindars and the rise of a new class of exploiters in the petty officials and clerks under the Government were the two dominant traits of nineteenth century Odishan social history. The contemporary Odia litterateur Fakir Mohan Senapati in his short story Rebati narrated 'how landlords, lawyers, shop keepers and even washermen hand like vultures over the wreck of human happiness".[36]

Odisha, during the period under discussion, witnessed a number of reforms. The British Government abolished the gruesome customs and evils in phases. The factors which prepared the ground for ushering in such changes were western influence and the impact of British rule, the role of the missionaries, the growth of education, the establishment of printing press and publications, socio-cultural activities and lastly, the development of communications.[37]

The social institutions such as Rammohan Ray's Brahmo Samaj, Dayanand Sarawati's Arya Samaj, Ranadey's Prarthna Samaj etc. also contributed significantly to remove blind-beliefs, superstitions and many a social evils from the Indian social evils and from the Indian social life.[38] In Odisha, many societies, associations and clubs came into existence in the 19th century. The roles of the socio-cultural associations like Cuttack Graduate Sabha, Balyabidhaba Nibarini Sabha, Aryaniti Sabha, etc, and the local journals and periodicals like Utkala Dipika and Sambalpur Hitaisini etc could not be set aside. Their principal aim was to bring about a general consciousness for social change.[39]

The role of the literature was also praiseworthy. The exploitations in the society and at the same time the desire to reform the then prevailing social process in Odisha was reflected in the writings of the contemporaries of Fakir Mohan Senapati. Fakir Mohan Senapati himself, through his foreceful literacy creations, highlighted the social evils and exploitations and tried to create consciousness among the masses. [40]

The rigorous caste system was whittled down by mass participation in the nationalist movement under Mahatma Gandhi's inspiration and enlightened liberalism. The nationalist movement of 1920s and 1930s, throwing men from several castes into the same jail and the rubbing of shoulders by political workers irrespective of caste considerations, took away a lot irritating patterns of iniquitous interactions between the high and low-castes in and outside the jails. The severest famine of 1866 in Odisha had also its impact on the lessening of the caste-rigour.[41]

The social reformation in Odisha was deeply influenced by the state of Bengal, which was the first to witness the flash of Indian renaissance. Calcutta, the Capital of British India at the time provided an ideal environment for the same.[53] "When the renaissance was taking place in Bengal, Odisha could not remain aloof from its spell as she happened to be a neighboring state. Furthermore, most of the Government servants and educated men in Odisha at the time were Bengalis. They acted as catalysts in accelerating social reactions and changes in Orissa.[42]

The social reforms of the 19th century like the abolition of sati brought about perceptible changes such as liberal attitude towards women and widows, and consequently widow-remarriage; abolition of child-marriage and promotion of women education. Suppression of infanticide brought respectability for women and female children of the Kondh tribes, in the course of suppressing meriah, the British Government promoted their economic status by construction of roads and establishment of schools and fairs. The consequent contact with Hindus organized their sanskritisation. The British Government was to be highly applauded for the manifold changes in the social lives of the people of Odisha. It was in the wake of social-reforms that the tribal began to prosper along with the inhabitants of the rest of Odisha. Undoubtedly, the social reforms of the 19th century Odisha provided a strong basis on which the social superstructure was built in the 20th Century.[43]

3.4 ECONOMIC CONDITION

During Fakir Mohan Senapati's time the economic condition of the people in Odisha was not up to the mark. By and large they were poor. Of course the economic condition varied from region to region and class to class. As regards the economic condition of the people, Dr. N.R. Patanaik observed:

If the standard of living was not up to the mark in Odisha it was mostly because of its people. Although the people's chief occupation in the plains was agriculture, the people living very close to the sea and the rivers earned their livelihood by making salt and catching fish. Many were also dependant on handicrafts, weaving and wood-cutting.[44]

In Saria and Bhagia, the weaver couple in *Six Acres and a Third*, we see an example of such dehumanisation brought about by extreme poverty.

First of all, they are uprooted from their traditional profession as weavers because of colonial economic policies. Subsequently, they are disinherited from their land and their cow, Neta, by Mangaraj. Saria dies of starvation and Bhagia turns mad and has to be confined in jail. It is not only the lives of this couple that are affected, *Six Acres and a Third* as a whole is a picture of chaos all around where Brahmin widows like Marua resort to prostitution, unscrupulous women like Champa rise to positions of power, and where Gobara Jena, the lumpen associate of Mangaraj, is beaten to death. *Six Acres and a Third* delineates a vast landscape of waste and death where both the oppressor and the oppressed succumb in their own contradictions. Even the moral voice of Santani is stifled into death. The contradictions spawned by the colonial world are so irresolvable that ultimately, they leave no survivors.

The economic standard of the tribal people, habituating in wild and forested regions, was altogether different. They were prone to self-indulgence and often got into debt and lost their lands. As such, in a large number of cases alienation of lands from the tribal people used to be affected by unfair and fraudulent means employed by the moneylenders.[45] A few tribes, the kondhs for example claimed an indefeasible right in the soil. However they constituted a restless wandering people who seldom remained long in the same spot.[46] But the tribes in general constituted a class of landless day laborers, the hewers of wood and clearers jungle who used to work for the superior Hindu castes.[47]

As a result of either drought or both, the people of Odisha witnessed some very serious famines. In the context Gould bury, the Commissioner of it, in his administrative report of Odisha, stated:

Odisha is subject to season's extreme uncertainty liable to most remarkable vicissitudes, of drought and inundation.[48]

During the British rule, famines occurred in 1806,1808, 1809,1817,1828,1836,1837,1842,1865,and1896. Scarcity was intensified during these years of famine by devastation and misgovernment of the rulers.[49] The Government even did not grant redemption of revenue in cases of natural calamities, which was usually done during the Maratha rule in Odisha (1751-1803).[50] However, the famine of 1865-66 has lagged behind the bitterest memories and is unparalleled in the annals of the Odisha history.[51] Hunter has thus rightly described that floods and famines in Orissa had loomed out like giant spectres from the dim panorama of the past.'[52]

The faulty land revenue administration of the British government was another important factor, which affected the economic condition of the people of Orissa especially the peasants. In this context Dr. P.C. Panda observed:

Unlike Bengal, in Odisha the Government often resorted to short term revenue settlements which resulted in utter ruination of the peasant community. Frequent short term settlements created prolonged unsettled and uncertain condition which served neither the interests of the peasants nor the state. Sympathy and sensibility of the administration was conspicuously lacking.[53]

The entire economy of Odisha of Fakir Mohan Senapati's time was thoroughly deranged due to the frequent droughts and floods, over-dependence on agriculture, faulty land revenue administration,lack of communication, non-utilization of natural resources and above all, mis governance and the rapacious attitude of the rulers.

3.5 CULTURAL BACKGROUND

The greatest contribution of Odisha to the Indian civilization is its cultural heritage. The culture of Odisha is identified with the all-embracing Jagannath culture. Thus Lord Jagannath's culture- which symbolizes universal brotherhood, harmony and fellow-feeling is the culture of Odisha. 'Two rivers have been flowing through Odisha and Odia nation: the first is Mahanadi and the second is Lord Jagannath. Like Jerusalem for the

Christians, Mecca for the Muslims, Puri – Jagannath is the ultimate goal for the Hindus. Puri- Jagannath is deemed to be the confluence of the people of all religions- Hinduism (Sakta Siva, Vaishnava, Ganapatya etc), Budhism and Jainism irrespective of caste, colour, creed and language.[54] The history of Odisha and Odia nation is built around Sri Jagannath.[55] Sri Samuel Ho, the then Secretary in charge of India, his ordinance-draft in British parliament for the formation of separate Odisha province, announced Odisha as 'the land of Lord Jagannath with one language, one religion and one race'.[56]

The art and architecture also formed an integral part of Odishan culture. The creative potentiality achievements of the Odias have been outstanding over the years and have been evident in their art, architecute, language and literature.[57] Odisha is a land of temples with their imposing architectural beauty which speaks volumes of the skill of the master masons of Odisha. The famous temples of Lord Jagannath at Puri and Lord Lingaraj at Bhubaneswar are known throughout the length and breadth of the country. The Sun-God temple at Konark is seven hundred years old and it represents the Sun-God standing in the time's winged chariot urging on his team of seven horses with which he blazes his way through the heavens.[58] Konark of Odisha is a living testimony to the speculative daring and the artistic sensibility of a force that once knew how to life, love and worship and create in heroic proportions.[59] The languages of man is defeated by the language of this stone.[60] Describing the superb artistic and architectural works on the hard surface of stones as well as slender palm leaves, Dr. M.N.Das has aptly said.

From the time of Ashoka's Dhauli and Kharavela's Kumari complex to the time of Konark, the Odishan sculptors and architects showed their calibre as a race of artists through generations and centuries. To a keen observer of the Mukteswar, the Rajarani or the Konark, the Orissan atists would appear to be playing with the needle as easily as the Ajanta painter played with his brush, for an exactitude which would need to erosion. And the themes were so varied for him, and his imagination so deep, he was, as if, writing an epic on the surface of stone.[61]

There are innumerable temples all over the state displaying marvels of art and architecture. The creativity and the originality of the Odias have also been expressed in the textile designs, silver filigree, palm-leaf painting and other artistic performances.[62]

Music and dance also contributed to flourish the Odishan culture. The Odishee dance is one of the most significant contributions of Odisha to the world of dance and music. The Odishan culture is highly enriched by the folk culture of the tribal dominated western region of Odisha. With an abundance of flora and fauna and varieties of birds and creatures around, the men of this region have developed a culture which is commonly known as Sambalpuri culture, which expresses itself in a special form of dialect, Sambalpuri – very close to the Odia language leaving apart the dialect, the various types of exotic folk songs and dances which exist in this area give ample evidence of its specialty and originality.[63]

During the time of Fakir Mohan Senapati with the development of nationalist movement certain material folk dances were revived to evoke the pride of the people in their glorious past.[64] However, in the absence of any official patronage the art of music and dance were kept alive mainly by the efforts of individual artists and certain societies.[65]

The language and literature of Odisha contributed significantly to enrich the Odishan culture. The language of Odisha is called 'Odia'. 'The influence of the various Indo-Aryans, Austric and Dravidian languages is clearly evident in the philological structure of the Odia language though the Sanskritic overtones are clearly perceptible. By the time of Fakir Mohan Senapati Odia as a language had already developed into its modern form. Odia as a literary language can be traced back to the vajrayani poets who wrote in apavransa- the precursor of modern Odia. Odia became the vehicle of literature as well as of state records by the 15th century.[66]

The language of Odisha was under great threat during Fakir Mohan Senapati's time. 'The partition of Orissa and her economic and political subservience to other regions placed Oriyas at disadvantage. They were reduced to the status of linguistic minorities in large administrative zones. Where the major language was Telgu, Hindi, or Bengali.'[67] As a result the Odias were compelled to adopt the majority language of their respective zones for administrative and educational purposes.

During that time there was attempt by some Bengali intellectuals to abolish Odia language from Odisha altogether. They treated Odia language as a dialect of the 'Bengali'. In the mid 19th century there was a movement in Calcutta demanding to include Bengali in place of Odia in the Schools of Odisha. Bengal's erudite Dr. Rajendralal Mitra and other Bengali intellectuals strongly and also very strangely supported this non-sense issue.[68] Of course, Gourishankar Ray- a Bengali by blood and an Odia by language and birth place, refuted the arguments of the Bengali erudite that Odia personalities of the time like Fakir Mohan Senapati, Gangadhar Meher. Madhusudan Rao, Gopabandhu Das, and a host of others to protect the dignity and originality of Odisha and Odia language.[69] Fakir Mohan Senapati's time is considred as the period of renaissance of Odia literature.[70]

New trends in Odia literature were introduced. The revolt against the old literacy conventions and the tendency to make new experiments in literary forms and techniques contributed a great deal in enriching Odia literature. The introduction of the printing press and wider circulation of newspapers and books also encouraged literary developments.[71] One of the important objectives of Odia literature of the time was also to protect and flourish Odia language.

Though Journalism was a spare- time, unpaid occupation, it played a crucial role in ushering a new age of awakening in Odisha of Fakir Mohan Senapati's time. In this regard Dr. C. Biswal observes:

Journalism, as an instrument of social change, was employed with utmost rigiour and force by two forceful editiors Viswanath Kar of 'The Utkal Sahitya' and Nilamani Vidyaratna of 'The Sambalpur Hitaisini' who through their forceful writings and balanced editorial policy, tried to arouse the dormant populace of the region.[72]

Gourishankar Ray also played a central role in the history of journalism in Odisha.[86] Establishment of printing press provided the much needed encouragement to both journalism and literature. The first printing press in Odisha was established in 1836 by Europian missionaries. The first indigenous publishing venture in Odisha was 'Cuttack Printing Company' which commenced operation on the 1st of July, 1865. The second Odia press Fakir Mohan Senapati & Co Utkal Press, was established by Fakir Mohan Senapati in Balasore in 1868, a Christian Press in Berhampur in 1876, a press in Mayurbhanj in 1881, the Puri Printing Company in 1882, the Jagannath Ballabha Press in Bamara in 1889, the Gajapati Press in Paralakhemundi in 1896, and a press in Talcher in 1896 were gradually established.[73] The successful launching of these indigenous printing presses throughout Odisha greatly assisted and activated journalism as well as the intellectual fermentation. Certainly, it added to the cultural transformation of Odisha.

Odia writter and educationalist Fakir Mohan Senapati was an active witness and not a mute spectator to the transformation of the Odia society. Fakir Mohan Senapati joined the ceaseless and concerted heroic and patriotic efforts to unify Odia people and to regenerate their cultural excellence.

3.6 PUBLIC INSTRUCTION

Odisha had an enriched tradition of education since time immemorial. 'Centres of learning were there at places like Toshali, Lalitgiri and Puspagir'[74] which speak volumes of the rich educational legacy of Odisha. The public instruction system in Odisha can be divided into two phases; indigenous education and western education. During Fakir Mohan Senapati's time both indigenous and western education run simultaneously.

3.6.1 INDIGENOUS EDUCATION

The indigenous education continued to prevail in Odisha during Fakir Mohan Senapati's time inspite of the introduction of western education system. There were a number of pathasalas (indigenous village Schools) in Odisha. Even before the British occupation. The teachers of such schools were called abadhans. Those pathasalas were privately managed. Normally the kings and zamindars were known to have employed Pundits or Gurus to teach their own children only.[75] The network of Bhagabata Tungi[76], also imparted non-formal cultural education to the common people.[77] Some mathas of Puri managed Sanskrit tols to impart various branches of Hindu learning.[78] Mr. E.Rhor, the Inspector of Schools of south west Division of Bengal Presidency, in 1857-58. Also observed the existence of some Sanskrit Tols.[79] Even the Muslims constituting less than two percent of population in Odisha had their own indigenous schools called maktabs and the teachers were called akhums.[80] Describing indigenous system of learning in Odisha, Hunter writes.

Here and there, indeed a Pundit taught a few lads Sanskrit in a corner of some rich landholder's mansions; and the larger villages had a sort of hedge-school, where half a dozen boys squatted with the master on the ground forming the alphabet in the dust, and repeating the multiplication table in a parrot-like sing song. Any one who could write a sentence. Two on a leaf passed for a man of letters.[81]

Mr. William Adams conducted systematic survey of the condition of indigenous education in Bengal Presidency, which also encompassed Odisha, and reported the existence of various types of schools, such as : elementary schools imparting the English system of education, elementary indigenous schools- established and supported by the villagers themselves and in which elementary knowledge was taught, indigenous schools of learning like the Sanskrit Tols imparting various branches of Hindu learning and the Arabic Madras as teaching the basics of Islam, and domestic schools conducted by private tutors and meant mainly for the children of a rich individual.[82]

According to Mr. Adams, every village had a school and mostly were open-air schools. The syllabus of such schools was confined to teaching the rudiments of literacy and numeracy. But the syllabus of English schools comprised of literacy and numeracy. But the syllabus of English schools comprised of reading, writing, arithmetic, grammer, geography, use of globes and general history. Teachers enjoyed a very low status and they were often ridiculed in public. The students had to pay an anna (one sixteenth of a Rupee) or two each per month as fees. The rich families employed the teachers as their servants.[83]

The state of public instruction in Odisha of Fakir Mohan Senapati's time is reflected in the literary works of his contemporaries like Gangadhar Meher, Madhusudan Das. Fakir Mohan Senapati, one of the pioneers of modern Odia literature, provided a concrete picture of the indigenous education system in his autobiography Atma Jibana Charita. His novels also reflect many aspects of the then education system. Though conservatism dominated the psyche of the people and militated against the acceptance of western education, the schools meant to impart western education were rapidly spreading. And at the same time there was declining trend in the position of indigenous schools known as Chatasali due to lack of due recognition and patronage.[84] As portrayed by Fakir Mohan Senapati 'the basic conception of and attitude towards education held by contemporary society was extremely narrow. Education was commonly regarded as synonymous with learning to read; and learning to read was an ability required only by those who were to earn a living by it.'[85] Regarding the educational facilities in the 1850s, Fakir Mohan Senapati observes:

> I was almost nine by the time I began attending school (Chatasali). There was a school to every big village in the district and one to every two or three small villages. The well-do-do engaged private tutors. The children of untouchables, used to sit a little way away from the upper-caste children.[86]

The indigenous education was teacher-centered. The abadhanas (teachers of indigenous schools) were be all and end all of the indigenous schools. Most of the teachers were Karanas by caste. They were mainly from Cuttack district. The teacher's were paid from students' donations (in kind) and gifts. Discipline was the most vital feature of the indigenous schools. Strict punishment such as- Standing on a single leg, nose- hair, kneeling etc. were meted out in schools; Even the students had to serve the teachers in domestic work after the study hours. A teacher's efficiency was normally judged by his capability to impose punishment on students. There were no printed text-books in Odia. The students were taught the arithmetic, specifically the Lilabati sutra (a treatise on Mathematics by Bhaskaracharya), reading of manuscripts, and writings of letters and petitions.[87] As regards the discipline in the indigenous schools, Fakir Mohan Senapati describe:

> Every single thing was against the rules in the Chatasali. There were rules for everyting, and transgression of them led to the inevitable punishment when you get tired of sitting in one spot you have to ask politely. Sir. One i.e. may I urinate? Sir, two: i.e. may I defecate? /Sir five 'may I have a drink of water.[88]

Fakir Mohan Senapati was dissatisfied with the western education current in Odisha in his days, for it produced only educated elite and tended to alienate this elite form its own society and culture. Fakir Mohan Senapati in his literary works, demonstated the need for education as an antidote to superstition and exploitation.[89] His literature also reflects the attitude of the contemporary society towards woman education. In his short story Rebati, when Rebati's grandmother hard of Rebati's education, she protested strongly.

What educate girls: whatever for? She must learn to cook and to serve a meal, to make a cake, decorate house and churn curbs: but reading? Never.[90]

Fakir Mohan Senapati's account of public instruction is supplemented by another contemporary of Meher and one of the chief architects of modern Odisha, Madhusadan Das (1848–1934). His unfinished autobiography presents an idea about the indigenous education of his time. As portrayed by Madhusudan Das, education was mostly a domestic affair for the rich and aristocratic families. Madhusudan Das himself received his elementary education from a private tutor. A teacher, who was qualified to read and write Odia and also knew arithmetic, was in charge of his elementary education, and received a monthly salary of Rs.7 in addition to food and clothing. His autobiography states nothing on the aspect of discipline. One of the interesting features, as evident from Madhusudan's own education, was the effort of the teachers to stimulate in children an interest in drawing and painting. The pupils were also taught how to write on palm – leaf, as it was the customary writing material in that days.[91] As regards the indigenous village schools, Madhusadan Das sums up:

In the village chatasalis one was taught to read, by writing in chalk on mud-floors. The teachers wrote characters on the floor and pupil read them aloud as he traced over them (with his chalk). The mud walls were used (like a black-board) for the teacher's calculations. For nothing down other information, and for drawing pictures of people animals and other scenes. These pictures were often very good. They were painted in red chalk, mixed with water and applied with the finger as a brush. They often served to stimulate in the children an interest in painting and fine arts.[92]

The survey conducted by William Adams and as well as the autobiographies of Gangadhar Meher, Madhusudan Das and Fakir Mohan Senapati himself depicted that indigenous education system did prevail in Odisha of Fakir Mohan Senapati's times in a very organized way.

3.6.2 WESTERN EDUCATION

The inroad of Western education was a significant feature of the public instruction in Orissa during the time of Fakir Mohan Senapati. Though the branch of education did not receive expected patronage form Government, the Christian Missionaries took the initiative and established schools in Orissa. The Baptist Mission was credited with establishing the first school imparting English education on 1st of June 1822 at Cuttack.[93] By December 1823; the Missionaries had established 15 schools in Odisha.[94]

The Education policy of 1835 enunciated by Lord Macaulay (Macaulay's Minutes) and approved by Lord Willam Bentick, marked a mile-stone for English education in India.[95] The adoption of Macaulay's minutes led to the sprouting of English schools in Odisha. Mr. W. Walkinson, the then Commissioner of Odisha, started the Puri English School on November 10, 1835. The school imparted education upto the Middle English school level.[96] The report of the General Committee of Public Instruction of Fort William in Bengal (1839-40) provides a brief idea about the class-I syllabus of the Puri English School which comprised Odia, Sanskrit, English grammar, History of England, Arithmetic and Geometry.[97]

It was on 18th march 1841, the Cuttack School was established, which became the first High School of Orissa in 1851. The School was renamed as Ravenshaw Collegiate School, after the name of the then Commissioner of

Odisha T.F.Revenshaw, in the year 1875. This school still exists and is the oldest institution of Odisha.[98] The Governor General Lord Hardinge proposed a scheme to establish 101 Vernacular Schools in the Presidency of Bengal, to impart elementary education through mother-tongue. Under this scheme 8 Vernacular schools were established in Odisha division in 1845. These Schools were located Puri, Balasore, Khurda, Bhadrak, Kendrapada, Remuna, Mahanga, and Hariharpur.[99] some ideas about the text books taught in the Schools of Odisha during 1842-47, are available from the report of the Department of Education relating to 'Kendrapada' and 'Mahanga' schools. In 1847-48, the text books and in these schools were:- Class-1: Odia Instructor, Geography, Vernacular reader and Grammar; Class- II: Odia Instructor, Grammar and Mathematics; Class-III : Writing and reading.[100] The syllabus for junior and senior scholarship examinations was amended in 1853. Accordingly a student has to opt for one of the vernaculars, such as- Bengali, Hindi, Urdu and Odia, apart from English. The textbooks prescribed for the junior English scholarship examination were Betala Panchavinsati and Tatwabodhani in Bengali; Vernacular Reader and Padarthavidyasara in Odia; and Moral Tales, Poetical Reader, History of England, Etymology, Grammar, Drawing, Algebra and Arithmetic in English.[101]

The Educational Despatch of 1854 of Chartles Wood, more commonly known as Wood's Despatch, was a land-mark in the history of western education in India. The Despatch, for the first time, introduced a regular grant-in-aid system to encourage people to establish private schools. It recommended vernacular as the medium of instruction in lower classes leading ultimately to higher education in English.[102] However, Odisha received no benefit from Wood's Despatch because the people were against the spread of English education.

The people not only take no interest in the welfare of the school, but many of them, it is said, entertain most absord notions of the intensions of

Government, believing that the children, if allowed to attend school, will eventually be taken away from their parents and sent to England.[103]

Odisha achieved some progress in the field of education due to the efforts of some Commissioners, the School Inspectors and Missionaries.[104] In 1854 for the first time a Directorate of Public Instruction was created in Bengal and Odisha was brought under its supervision. It was only in 1874 a separate Inspectorate of education for Odisha was created.[105] The first English school was established in Ganjam as late as 1858 i.e. full fifty years posterior to the date when the other districts of Madras had come under the enlightening influence of English education.[106]

In 1858-59 there were 22 Government schools and 8 Aided schools in Odisha. Out of these 30 schools, 25 were Vernacular schools as well. By 1863- 64 of the number of Schools increased to 44, out of which 24 were Government schools and 20 were Aided schools, The 24 Government schools included three district level schools, called Zilla schools, one each at Cuttack, Puri and Balasore, Cuttack Normal school and 20 Vernacular schools.[107] The Vernacular schools located at rural areas received grant-in-aid through local committees. The Zilla schools at Cuttack was upgraded to the status of High school in 1867.[108]

It was after the creation of the 'Province of Bihar and Odisha' that the expansion of education gained momentum. The Primary Education Act which was passed in 1919 made primary education compulsory in the province, and resulted in further expansion of education. It was first introduced in 1921 in Ranchi and later extended to Banki rural area in Cuttack district of Odisha Division in 1923.[109]

There were two types of Middle schools: Middle Vernacular schools and middle college English schools. The Middle vernacular schools were placed under the control of the District Boards and Municipalities, which managed these institutions directly in urban areas.[110] Prior to 1870, education in Middle vernacular Schools was imparted through Odia, whereas in the Middle English school, the medium of instruction was English. But in 1870-71, in order to bring uniformity in both Middle Vernacular Schools and Middle English schools.Provision for teaching both Odia and English was made in both types of schools. It was done only after the Culcutta University made it compulsory for students to write every subject in English in its Entrance examination in 1861-62. During 1912-13 there were 9 Middle Englsih schools in Odisha, which received financial grant directly from Government. In 1917, twenty four new Middle English schools were opened. The demand of parents and pupils alike for English education resulted in the conversion of a large number of Middle Vernacular schools as Middle English schools. During 1916-17 there were 130 Middle schools which rose to 514 by the year 1925-26.[111]

The Odisha Division had only 8 High schools in 1913. The number increased to 10, with the establishment of two High Schools, one each at Sambalpur and Angul, in the year 1926. The Provincial Government introduced High School Leaving Certificate Examination in 1920. Again in the year 1923, the Board of Secondary Eduction was created in the province of Bihar and Orissa to conduct examinations, and inspect the secondary schools.[112]

The Provincial Government of Bengal ignored Odisha Division in providing facilities for higher education. It was due to the initiative of Mr.M.R.L.Martin, Inspector of Schools of South –West Division, and T.E.Ravenshaw the then Commissioner of Odisha, that two college classes were opened in Cuttack High school in 1868. This College was upgraded to the status of a first class college, and the Cuttack High school got its separate existence in year 1878. The first and foremost college in Odisha was named as Ravenshaw college' after the name of T.E.Revenshaw.[113]

The Normal school meant for teacher- training was first established at Cuttack in Odisha Division in 1863, and was recognized from the beginning of 1869. The Normal school was placed under the charge of a

Superintendent. It had two departments : Pundit Training and Guru Training. The former was a two years course and the later a one year course. [114]

The development of vocational education was also very negligible in Odisha. It was in the year 1876 that a medical school was established at Cuttack.[115] A survey school was also opened at Cuttack in the same year. And after a long gap of forty-seven years, the Odisha School of Engineering was established at Cuttack in July, 1923.[116]

The progress of education was much slower in the western hilly region of Odisha as compared to that in the coastal plains.

Thus Fakir Mohan's conservatism was not in conflict with what was beneficial in modernity. It was somewhat like the conservatism of Bhudev Mukhopadhyaya, a leading contemporary Bengali intellectual who believed that "India should learn from Europe nothing but her 'practical skills' and absorb these into her inherited culture in a gradual, organic fashion" (Raychoudhuri Fakir Mohan echoed this kind of tactical conservatism which had a strong radical edge. Both believed that true modernity cannot be mediated under a hegemonic dispensation. However, since Bhudev operated throughout his life within an elite circle he did not have the scope to experience the oppressiveness of colonial structures from the position of a disempowered subject. Fakir Mohan had experienced the colonial hegemony from various subject positions due to the peculiarity of his circumstances as narrated earlier. Therefore, he was in a position to provide a plan of action through which his vision could be actualised. The novel was a part of that plan of action, for through the novel he tried to create "active readers" (Sawyer) who could be instruments in the act of ungrafting colonialism and establishing the "Swarajya" or autonomy of consciousness. Fakir Mohan sincerely believed that reading the novel was one of the means of reading colonialism and the active reader can make the transition from the text to the world through the act of interpretation, the kind of which we had a glimpse in the *Six Acres and a Third* mentioned in the beginning of the essay.

From the foregoing analysis it can be observed that the indigenous as well as western education continued to exist with each other. Although there were facilities of western education, Fakir Mohan Senapati's own education was limited to the scope of indigenous education only. Poverty and lack of communication are said to be the reasons for his failure to pursue western education.

REFERENCES

1. C.B.Biswal, A study of the contribution of Radhanath Rai and Madhusudan Rao in the 19th century educational situation in Orissa, Upanishad, Ph.D thesis, Sambalpur University, 1989, PP.20-21.
2. N. C. Behuria (ed), Orissa State Gazzetter, Vol1, Bhubaneswar: Government of Orissa. 1990,P.3
3. C. Biswal, op.cit, PP.21-22.
4. N. C. Behuria(ed), op.cit, P.10.
5. W. Hamilton, A geographical, Statical and Historical Description of Hindustan and its adjacent countries, Vol.II, London, 1820, P.32.
6. N. R. Pattnaik, Social history of 19th century Orissa, Allahabad, 1989, PP.3-5
7. Ibid, PP.6-7
8. Ibid, PP.9-17
9. N. Pattnaik and C. Pradhan, The Oriya movement, Cuttack: Bharat Bharati Publication, 1919, P.32.
10. Calcutta Gazzette Supplement, 23.10.1895, P.2357.
11. Ibid, P.37.
12. B. Mohapatra, Odia Andolanara Itihas, Cuttack, 1976, PP. 54-58.
13. Ibid, P.VIII
14. Para 20 of the Harding Dispatch, Dated 25 August,1911.
15. Utkal Dipika (Weekly), Cuttack, 24.4.1912 and 20.7.1912.
16. Report of the Indian Statutory Commission, Vo.IV, 1930, p. 538
17. P. C. Panda, op. cit, PP.VII-XII.
18. N. C. Behuria(ed), op.cit, PP.226-227.
19. Annual report on Newspapers, Govt. of Bihar and Orissa, Political special, file No. 144 and 163 of 1921
20. P.C.Panda, op.cit,P.91.
21. N.C.Behuria(ed), op.cit, PP.227-233.
22. Ibid.PP.227-228

23. P.C.Panda, op.cit,PP.34-40.
24. N.C.Behuria(ed), op.cit, PP.227-233.
25. R.Patnaik, op.cit, PP.29-36.
26. Sati was a short of religious suicide prevailed among high caste Hindus in which windows sacrificed their lives on the funeral pyres of their husband, which the nation that they would accompany their husband to other world.
27. Meriah is a short of human sacrifice to the Earth Goddess, Kali performed by the Kondh tribes, since they called the victim meriah, this practice was popularly known as meriah sacrifice or simply meriah.
28. N. R. Patnaik, op.cit, P.293.
29. N. Patnaik and C.Pradhan,, op.cit, P.91.
30. L.L.S.O.Malley, Bengal, Bihar, Orissa, Sikkim, Cambridge, 1917, P.185.
31. N. C.Behuria(ed), op.cit, PP.296-300.
32. N.Patnaik and C.Pradhan, op.cit, P.93.
33. F. M. Senapati, Fakir Mohan Granthavali, Vol-I, Cuttack, 1963, PP. 545-546.
34. A. Kavi, Kara Kavitare Gopabandhu, Konark, No.33, Bhubaneswar Orissa Sahitya Acadamy, 1977, PP.120-136.
35. N.R.Patnaik, op.cit, P.278.
36. J. V. Boulton, Fakir Mohan Senapati: His life and prose fictions, Bhubaneswar Orissa Sahitya Acadamy, 1993, P.276.
37. N. R. Patnaik, op.cit, 1966, PP.37-55.
38. N. Pradhan(ed), Gangadhar Granthavali, Cuttack: Dharmagrantha Store, 1966, P.77.
39. N. R. Patnaik, op.cit, PP.276-284.
40. N. Pradhan(ed), op.cit, PP.77-78.
41. N. C. Behuria (ed), op.cit, PP.288-289.
42. D.Kopf. British Orientalism and Bengal Renaissance, Calcutta, 1969, P.283.
43. N.R.Patnaik, op.cit, P.43.
44. Ibid, P.19.

45. Report of the Partially excluded areas enquiry committee Orissa, Cuttack, 1940, P.19.
46. Central Provinces Gazzetter, Nagpur, 1870,P239.
47. W.W.Hunteer, op.cit, P.69.
48. C.Biswal, op.cit, P.26.
49. N.Patnaik and C.Pradhan, op.cit, P.180.
50. G.Toynbee, "A sketch of history of Orissa (1803-1828), Orissa historical research journal, Vol.IX, No-1&2, 1960,PP.42-45.
51. C.Biswal, op.cit, P.26.
52. W.W.Hunteer, op.cit, P.174.
53. P.C.Panda, op.cit, P.46.
54. J.P.Singh Deo, Origin of Jagannath Deity, New Delhi:Gyan Publishing House, 1991,P.15
55. P.Adhikari(ed), Ama Jagannath Ama Sanskruti, Cuttack, 1981, P.19
56. Ibid.P.86
57. J.Mohanty, Childrens literature of Orissa, Bhubaneswar, Orissa sahitya academy, 1993, P.5.
58. S.Nanda, Coalitional politics in Orissa, New Delhi, Sterling publishers Pvt, Ltd. 1979, P.4
59. Ibid.
60. Justice H.R.Khanna reportof the commission of Enquiry, 1968,P.807.
61. J.Mohanty, op.cit, PP.5-6.
62. Ibid,P.6
63. S.C.Pujhari,Drums of Sambalpur, Odisha lokanrutya O sangita mohatsov, Sambalpur, PP,5-6.
64. Ibid, P.8.
65. C.Raychoudhury, Social cultural and economic history of India, New Delhi, 1978, PP.227-241.
66. C.Biswal, op.cit, P.28.
67. J. V. Bulton, op. cit, P.22.
68. M. Mansingh, Odia Sahityara Itihas, cuttack: Granthamandir Publication, 1967, P.206.
69. J.V.Bulton, op.cit, PP.59-95.

70. C. Biswal, op.cit, PP.28-29.
71. C. Raychoudhury, op.cit, PP.206-225.
72. C. Biswal, op.cit, PP.28-29.
73. J.V.Bulton, op.cit, P.37.
74. Ibid, PP.24-35.
75. C. Biswal, op.cit, P.34.
76. Bhagavata Tungi is a religious village club where Bhagabata, a Hindu religious scripture written by Jagannath Das, which is full of moral instruction is recited every evening to the villagers who gather irrespective of caste, creed and colour.
77. C.Biswal, op.cit, PP.34-35.
78. W.Adams, Report on the state of education in Bengal, 1835 and 1838, University of Calcutta, 1941, P.54.
79. General report on public instruction in the lower provinces of Bengal presidency, 1857-58,P.115.
80. N.R.Pattnaik, op.cit,P.58.
81. W.W.Hunter, op.cit,P.145.
82. C.Biswal, op.cit, PP.37-38.
83. Ibid,PP.36-41.
84. J.V.Boulton, op.cit,P.22.
85. Ibid,P.340.
86. C.Biswal, op.cit, PP.45-50.
87. J.V.Boulton, op.cit,P.341.
88. Ibid,PP.336-337.
89. Ibid,P.349.
90. Ibid,PP.344-346.
91. Ibid,P.344.
92. P.K.Patra, Odishare Baptist Missonary Societyra Karya, Baptist Mission press, 1943, P.22.
93. N.Samabtaray, Odisha sahityara itihas, Cuttack, 1964,PP.46-47.
94. H.Sharp(ed), Selection from education records (1781-1839),part-I, Calcutta, 1908, P.127.

95. V.B.Shastry, Development of secondary education in Orissa, (1882-1966), unpublished Ph.D. thesis, Utkal University, 1980, P.44.
96. Report of the general committee of public instruction of Fort willim in Bengal, 1839-40,PP.64-65.
97. C.Biswal, op.cit, P.82.
98. Report of the council of education, 1844-45,APPX-2,PP.CLXIX-XI
99. Report of the council of education,1847-78, P.180.
100. General report of public instruction, 1852-55,PP.CCXCIX and CCXXV
101. N.R.Pattnaik, op,cit,PP.63-64.
102. Ibid.P.59.
103. S.C.Patra, The formation of the province of Orissaq, Calcutta, 1979, P.80.
104. W.W.Hunter, op.cit,PP.145-146.
105. N.Patnaik and C.Pradhan, op.cit, P.32.
106. N.Samantray, op.cit,PP.46-47.
107. P.C.Panda, op.cit,PP.86-89.
108. Annual Administrative report, Bihar and Orissa, 1927-28, P.35.
109. Annual Administrative report, Bihar and Orissa, 1924-25, P.99.
110. P.C.Panda, op.cit,PP.86-90.
111. Ibid.PP.90-92.
112. The Orissa historical journal, Vol.XII,No.1, 1964, P.27.
113. C.Biswal, op.cit, PP.60-61.
114. N.Patnaik, op.cit, PP.450-451.
115. Ibid.PP.88-92.
116. N.Samantray, op.cit, P.91.

♦♦♦

CHAPTER-IV

LIFE SKETCH OF FAKIR MOHAN SENAPATI

CHAPTER IV

LIFE SKETCH OF FAKIR MOHAN SENAPATI

4.1 FAMILY BACKGROUND

Fakir Mohan Senapati was born on Friday, the 14th of January 1843 or 1250 of the Saka era in the village of Malikashpur to the town of Balasore. His father was Laxman Charan Senapati and mother Tulsi Dei. On his birth one golden ring was put on his ear by making a hole through it, because his elder brother died before him. People had belief that after the death of the elder son, if there would be a hole in the ear as a next son, he was not to be taken by Yama. But Fakir Mohan lost his parents before he was two years old.[1]

The title conferred on Hanu Malla by the Marathas was 'Senapati' (General). His unworthy descendant forsook their family name Malla and through landless and armyless, have continued to use the title 'Senapati' ever since. His relationship to Hanu Malla is shown in the following family tree. [2]

Hanu Malla(Senapati)
↓
Govinda Malla(Senapati)
↓
Kusa Malla(Senapati)
↓
Purusottama Senapati | Laksmana Carana Senapati
↓
Fakir Mohan Senapati

The first of his ancestors to move to Balasore was Hanu Malla when young had enlisted with the Marathas as a fool-soldier. His job was to guard the Phulbar pass against the Pathans. As pay he was granted nine hundred acres of tax free land. He was then the commander of a large number of foot-soldier, who also held tax-free land in lieut of pay. Their descendants continued in undisputed possession of these lands until the first settlement in 1843 by which time some of the families had died out. Those who could still produce deeds, were confirmed in their ownership, whilst those who could not, lost possession. [3]

4.2 CHILDHOOD

Fakir Mohan Senapati had heard that at birth his left ear was pierced and a gold ring inserted. He had an elder brother named Chaitanya Carana. He had passed away before he was born. There was a superstition that when an elder son died, the next son should have his ear pierced at birth, because then death would disdain to take him away. In his childhood he met hundreds of others with similarly pierced ears.

When Fakir Mohan Senapati was seventeen months old his father went to Puri to see Lord Jagannatha's Car Festival. He was attacked with cholera and died at Bhubaneswar on his way home. He had been accompanied by a number of fellow-villagers and his mother, Kuchila Dei, Fakir Mohan's granny. Granny told Fakir Mohan that father died on the stone steps of Bindu Sagar, a tank near the temple in Bhubaneswar. People wept when news of his father's death reached the village, his father's pet dog had began moaning in harmony with the general lament, and continued to do so after the others had ceased. Father used to visit in the village and all the spots where he used to sit. After fretting for eight whole days without touching food, it died.

On hearing of her husband's death Fakir Mohan's Mother took to her bed and never left it. For fourteen months she suffered intense mental and physical anguish and then died on the eighth day of bright in the month of Bhadrab (August–September) in the year 1252 of the Sana era i.e. 1845 A.D.

After the death of Fakir Mohan's mother, he was confined to bed for seven or eight years with disagreeable maladies like diarrhoea and piles. Granny watched over him day and night, for what must have been months and years – for much of the time without food and sleep- as if in an eternal tug- of-war with death who hung on tenaciously to one of his hands, whilst she pulled the other. Finally he triumphed, and began to convalesce.

After Fakir Mohan parent's death as if at the Lord's command, my grandmother, Kuchila Dei, Began nursing me. We have a local saying: 'if mother doesn't raise them, dad's mother will'. It saddens Fakir Mohan to recall even dimly how his grand mother struggled and suffered to save Fakir Mohan, even if unable to repay a fraction of her kindness to me. [4]

After the death of his parents, he was brought up by his grandmother, Kochila Dei. The role of father and mother was played by his uncle. Purusottam Senapati and his grandmother respectively. Till the age of eight he had to suffer this irrevocable agony. During that period, his grandmother served for him and saved his life from death in order to suffer for this irrevocable agony. During that period. In order to cure him she called two Muslim piras of Balasore. She made a vow before them that "after the recovery of my child Braja, I will make him your Fakir," "Fakir" (Muslim mendicant).[5] Miraculously, the boy originally named Braja Mohan recovered and became known as Fakir Mohan. There after, he was made a "Fakir" for eight days during Muharram of Ramjan month every year and offered "Simi" at Pir Dargha with whatever he received as alms during that period. Thus Hindu God and Muslim Pir joined hands to keep alive Fakir Mohan, who latter emerged as a novelist of rare caliber not only in Odia language but also in Indian literature.

The name Fakir Mohan itself implies the fusion of both Muslim and Hindu communities. Besides that, his life is also a glaring example of Muslim impact on Hindu culture.

Fakir Mohan was born to suffer, it was only a doting grandmother's affectionate care that saved the sickly, pale and jaundiced child from immanent death to fulfill her vow she earned for himself the name Fakir Mohan's name was Braja Mohan But his grandmother gave him the name Fakir after his recovery from the disease. [6]

4.3 EDUCATION

At the age of nine Fakir Mohan received his early education in the village school. The time when he entered the school, There was neither any printing press nor text books nor were there writers and readers. Even the existence of Odia as a language was being doubled and questioned by people at the helm of educational affairs.[7]

In the school besides education he had to serve for his teacher. Baishnab Mohanty was helping him to prepare his meal. Later on, Fakir Mohan was admitted into the pathashala of "Nanda Gosain Matha" in his own village. Then he admitted himself into a Parsee School at Balasore. There he learnt how to write letters and applications. Fakir Mohan also went to village school teacher, Harekrushna of Sovarampur, to learn "Lilabati Sutra". But when the teacher did not teach him the same formula he was compelled to stop going there.[8]

Fakir Mohan secretly obtained admission in the Mission School at Barabati of Balasore town. There he studied history, geography and mathematics. He impressed his teachers with his talents. But he discontinued his education there because he became unable to pay only 25 paisa per month as the school fees. At home, he had jealous and unkind uncle and aunt. So home was a hell to him. Fakir Mohan learnt English through self-labour. He took the help of a dictionary to read some famous classics such as the Arabian Nights, Robinson Crusoe, the English Bible, and Bengal Peasant Life by Lai Behari De. Although he started learning English at the age of 23, his innate brilliance of mind was recognised even by foreigners.

Down to the sixties of the last century. Balasore was an important port in the east coast of India for the sailing ships of the East India Company, The father and the uncle of Fakir Mohan were engaged in this shipping work at Balasore port which was a profitable business. Fakir Mohan had been withdrawn from the village primary school on account of extreme poverty and made to earn his living by watching the repair of sails and rigging on behalf of his uncle who had many contractors for such jobs on the quarry side. He worked there as a Gomasta mate. At the end of the shipping works, he switched on to the salt depots at Bhuin Sahi, near Balasore. It was probably this hard and unfortunate childhood that made him a humanitarian and lover of children throughout his life.[9]

4.5 FAMILY LIFE

At the age of thirteen, Fakir Mohan married Lilabati Devi daughter of Narayana Parida of Manikakhumba, by the order of his uncle Purosottam Senapati. When Fakir Mohan was twenty-nine his wife died, leaving a daughter named Sarojini Senapati. His first wife was, according to his own candid confession quarrelsome, cruel and hard-hearted. He says,"My married life was more painful to me than the agonies of childhood."[10] It called to mind that old Sanskrit saying:

> "A man whose mother is not at home
> And whose wife is sharp-tongue
> May as well live in the jungle,
> For jungle and home are the same to him".

From his second wife Krushna Kumari Dei, Fakir Mohan had his only son Mohini Mohan Senapati. Sarojini Senapati married to Gagan Bihari Chaudhuri who was the then Dist Judge at Cuttack. Gagan Behari Chaudhari had three sons and one daughter they were Bipin Bihari Chaudhury, Saila Bihari Chaudhury and Snehamayee Devi. Snehamayee Devi who married to Suryamani Jena, a graduate from Calcutta University was the Inspector of Schools. Even the Senior Advocate and former Law Minister late Mr. Ashok Sen and his elder brother were the students of Suryamani Jena at Sambalpur High School. Surya Mani had three sons and one daughter namely Pratap Chandra Varma, Ajay Chandra and Sanjaya Chandra Varma. Prasanta Varma, Advocate Supreme Court of India was the son of late Mr. Pratap Chandra Varma and was one of the Great Grand Son of Fakir Mohan Senapati. Fakir Mohan's great-grand-daughter Monica Das was a writer and economist based out of New Delhi, India.

Actually Fakir Mohan's consolation was his Granny. When she died, his home life become unbearable.

According to Fakir Mohan Senapati, "my second wife delivered me from all domestic trouble and distress and to improve my fortune, comfort and prosperity, merciful God sent me Krushna Kumari Dei as a wife. She possessed all the virtues in full measure: truthfulness, loyalty and piety. She deemed her highest duty. At the time of second wedding of Fakir Mohan, Krushna Kumari Dei was only eleven years old, She died in 1894, leaving a son.

Actually Fakir Mohan's constant loneliness was his destiny. In childhood, he was an orphan.In youth he was in far away places separated from his wife and even in his old age he was alone, parted from his son. Solitude afforded him plenty of time for reflections. He was not good at work, because of his constant illnesses, but time of illness and stress seemed to improve his writing. During these long years of loneliness, Fakir Mohan was granted peace by Krushna Kumari Dei's tomb in his garden. That garden was called 'Santi Kanana'. Cradled in this peaceful solitude, Fakir Mohan composed the last works of his life, Mamu, Prayaschitta,

Bauddhavatara Kavya and very much important work, "Atma Jivana Charita".

In 1899, Fakir Mohan went to Kendrapara on the invitation of Zamindar Laxminarayan Jagdev. He reached there to save him from the debts which were incurred by him for religious work and guest entertainment . He remained there for nine months to save the Zamindari from its run but failed . When the Zamindar refused to reduce the expenses for religious work. Fakir Mohan left for Cuttack. In 1905, Fakir Mohan came to Balasore and resided in his "Shantikanan" residence.

In 1909, Fakir Mohan was saved luckily in spite of taking undiluted sulphur acid mistaken for medicine which was given to him by his "Gomasta" Srikantha Pattanaik . Again after two years he suffered form a pimple on his back. During that period. Maharaja Baikunthanath De of Balasore visited "Shantikanan" residence of Fakir Mohan, but the Maharaja died at Calcutta before Fakir Mohan's Death. His successor, Manmath Nath De, took care of Fakir Mohan, Other persons like Maulai Asraf Ali Kavyaratna. Mrutunjay Kavyatirtha Banibhusan and Gopabandu Das came to see Fakir Mohan. On the death-bed of Fakir Mohan, Gomasta Srikantha, gardener Jagamohan and maidservant Ketaki were helpful to him.

In his last life , Fakir Mohan was disgusted with his son, Mohini Mohan, suffering continuously from physical pain and mental anguish, So he disallowed him as his son. He had formed a trust by making a will. The will contains the descriptions to donation and feasting to be held on the death anniversary of his last wife krushana Kumari, maintenance of "Shantikanan", and peasant for his old Gomasta Srikantha, and help for his son's and his three granddaughter's education till their marriage and to make arrangement for his would be grandson's heir ship to all the property, and the authority of the girls school of Balasore to take aid if the smooth discharge of their duty to be hampered.

In 1916, Raja Sachidananda Tribhuban Dev of Barhmanada gave the title "Saraswati" to the 12th session of the Utkal Union Conference at Balasore, Fakir Mohan himself addressed the conference in December 1916 holding stick in his hand.

Towards the end of 1917, Fakir Mohan presided over the meeting of Utkal Sammilani held at Cutack in ill health. Madhusudan Das's remarks were that once the seat of the president of Utakal Sammilani was occupied as the Maharajas, today that seat was given to a Fakir Mohan. It was the last meeting for him and he told in the meeting that, he was taking farewell from the people of this country. Literally, he passed way from this world on 14 June 1918.

4.5 FAKIR MOHAN AS A TEACHER

Extreme poverty compelled Fakir Mohan to give up studies and to earn his living. He narrated in his autobiography that he could not pay four annas per month as tuition fee of the school though he was promoted to next higher class securing the first position. As there was no work for him he sat silently at home.[11]

A post of teacher was lying vacant or created due to the increase of student strength in Barabati School. The secretary of the school was Siba Chandra Soom. By his own experience, he knew that Fakir Mohan gave up his study for non payment of the tuition fee. He knew the spirit Fakir Mohan had possessed. Though Fakir Mohan had no educational certificate, and the time of his education was more than two and a half years, still Siba Chandra Soom gave appointment to unemployed Fakir Mohan as the third teacher in Barabati School with the monthly salary of two and a half rupees. [12]

This amount was increased to four rupees from the third month of his service. That day boy labour became a teacher, the importance was that he was not a labourer, he was a serviceman. He had little education in comparison with other teachers of Barabati School. The extraordinary ability, deftness and incision which Fakir Mohan had shown in his life as an assistant teacher first, and then as headmaster was not seen in the life of other qualified school and college teachers. The young and half-educated Fakir Mohan taught geography in first and second classes at Barabati School. As teacher he soon distinguished himself in an incident. There was no map in Barabati School; sometimes the maps were brought from Balasore Zilla School only to manage the study of the student. But Fakir Mohan prepared a map by his own hand in order to teach geography well to the students. The first hand made map of Fakir Mohan was American Continent which was the first own map of Barabti school. Fakir Mohan was praised by the secretary of the school and the Deputy Inspector of Schools for his hazardous work which he had done for the betterment of the students. As a result, the salary of Fakir Mohan was increased to five rupees per month. [13]

Without taking the advice of others or looking for a certified headmaster and assistant teacher of Barabati school, Reverend A. Miller secretary of Balasore Mission School appointed Fakir Mohan as the headmaster with the monthly salary of ten rupees in 1864.In course of time the headmastership in the mission school paved the way of Fakir Mohan's promising future. For this ten rupees service, the social importance of Fakir Mohan reached so high a place that nobody could have dreamt of that. The boy labour occupied the highest social place in Balasore town. [14]

During his service in Mission School for the first time he came in contact with Christian missionaries and the British officers. Perhaps the Britishers were more quality-lovers than the Indians. Otherwise how could a certificate less non-Christian get the post of headmaster in a missionary school? The secretary of the Mission school was a short-tempered man. He did everything which would come to his mind. Any proposal given to him by Fakir Mohan for the betterment of the school produced the reverse effect . Differences began to grow between Fakir Mohan and the secretary R.A.Miller on the issue of the correction of the translated book. Miller was informed that Fakir Mohan destroyed the translated book writing unholy words. It was believed by Miller as Fakir Mohan was a Hindu. As a result, Fakir Mohan left the school. [15]

Leaving Mission school Fakir Mohan got a non-official engagement. He taught Bengali language to R.H. Passi, the temporary Collector of Balasore and Mayers, the joint magistrate of Balasore. For the kindness of the Collector. Fakir Mohan was appointed as Munsi in the Collectorate. He remained in the post for some days. But this service was not suited to Fakir Mohan. When Reverend E.C.B.Hallam joined as the new secretary of mission school. On his request again Fakir Mohan joined in the precious writer. Hallam acquired a good knowledge in Odia language. He wrote an Odia English grammar book. Fakir Mohan helped him a lot for the completion of the book for which the name of Fakir Mohan was written in that grammar book . [16]

Fakir Mohan wrote one book on Odia grammar and another on arithmetic. These two books were grammar for the course in the school, with the help of grammar and dictionaries he began to read assiduously Sanskrit and English, and in no time acquired proficiency in no less than five languages. With the permission of lswar Chandra Vidyasagar. He translated the book jidan charita from Bengali to Odia. Ha was paid by the school with seven hundred rupees and three hundred rupees by the school inspector and the commissioner of Odia respectively . [17]

The secretary of the mission school increased the salary of Fakir Mohan from ten rupees to twenty five rupees for the better result of the school. In the first year class, four students passed and three were selected to get scholarship of four rupees. As a result, the mission school occupied the first position in Odisha. [18]

For the good fortune of Fakir Mohan, John Beams came to Balasore as the new collector and he was a great linguist. He had good knowledge of eleven languages for which he was in need of assistance of someone, who had a good knowledge of Bengali, Odia and Sanskrit. Hallam introduced Fakir Mohan to John Beams. A turning point in the life of Fakir Mohan was when he met with John Beams. On the first meeting john Beams asked some questions with the answer. Through sheer mental brilliance, efficiency, the semi educated Fakir Mohan established intimate friendship with Britishers of the highest rank. Fakir Mohan met John Beams once in a week and the discussion went on Sanskrit sloka, Bengali poems, Mantras on snake and Dahani etc. [19]

Johan Beams the collector of Balasore, wrote about Fakir Mohan Senapati, "He had however, left it for the better post of Dewan senapati, in which capacity I am glad to see he is carrying out improvements and introducing those principles of honesty and justice which he has imbibed from the teaching of the late Dewan. This is one out of many instances of the vast amount of indirect good done by the excellent man whose loss we all deeply deplore". [20]

4.6 FAKIR MOHAN AS A JOURNALIST

The name of Fakir Mohan spread all over Odisha as a good teacher and writer of text books. This fame made him as the leader of the whole Odia race. Fighting against odds, he thought to bring prestige to his own language and race. He himself dedicated his heart and soul for the spread and development of his own language, when he was the teacher at Balasore. At an early age, the prime aim of Fakir Homan was to improve Odia as mother tongue. [21]

By the year 1868, there was much availability of Bengali text books. A number of Bengali journals were published. The Bengalis had the pride that they enjoyed all power and privilege over this vast land. They came to believe that they were the pioneering genius in India. The Odias, Biharis and Assamese were inferior and they were headless, history-less and reckless. The territories of Odisha, Bihar and Assam were under the Bengal Presidency, so the educated Bengalis preached that all the historical monuments were the achievements of Bengalis, even the Bengalis began to criticize the Odias, Biharis and Assamese openly in order to establish the importance and prestige of their nation. [22]

The publication of the Bengali journals inspired Fakir Mohan to become a journalist to improve Odia language. If there would be no development of one's mother tongue, the nation would be ignored for good, and in apprehension of this, he was determined to make all efforts for the development of the mother tongue. He thought day and night for the improvement of his own language He wrote, "With a new book in hand I turn over its pages for a long time and I thing when such a book in Odia will come out. Reading other periodicals and journals he dreamt of publishing those types of journals in Odia. [23]

Madhusudan Das and Fakir Mohan both were harassed by the criticism of the Bengalis although they rose to highest place by their extraordinary quality. They narrated the painful story of the Bengali supremacy which they had suffered in their young. Fakir Mohan wrote: "Hence, forward the remarks made the Bengali Babus are intolerable. I cannot remain silent the way in which the Bengali teacher and other Bengali Babus give remarks sarcastically while mentioning Odia language, indeed I feel like showing my worth and hear-felt anguish towards the condemners as if they were offending our mother. It is my thought night and day and the sole aim that by any means we have to sacrifice ourselves for the sake of development of the mother tongue. At that time I was aged only nineteen or twenty. Again I had the lack of learning, lack of strength and a pauper." [24]

In order to remove the offence to the mother tongue, Fakir Mohan wrote a number of books, but these were only meant for the students. He thought that the mother tongue would develop only when the common people would read the printed books. The first step in this line was to print and to sell the books on ancient Odia literature. Then the people would read these printed books. Other books would be printed later on from the profit of the sales. And gradually the people would be habituated to reading the printed books.

The printing was not easy. A good amount of money was required for the printing. For this reason, the first book of Fakir Mohan 'Rajput rare Itishas' was not to he printed when the Mission Press of Cuttack estimated the printing charge of the book at the three hundred rupees. For the improvement of Odia literature , through Fakir Mohan's encouragement, a committee was constituted in Balasore town for the first time in the history of modern Odisha. The committee was constituted with six members and Fakir Mohan was one of them. The Committee first selected to print 'Rasakallola' of Dinakrushna Das. So a joint company was formed to collect money for printing which amounted to two hundred fifty rupees. The committee faced a problem that , after the printing of ' Rasakallola' how many years were to be spent for the printing of other books, because the selling of books should take time. Printing of enough books every year would develop the Odia literature quickly. [25]

It was decided to establish a printing press on the lines of printing company of Cuttack which was established by Gouri Shankar Roy on joint stock basis. Unassociated with the government in any way. Fakir Mohan all by himself , was the pioneer in propaganda for the cooperative movement which was just reaching this country from the west. [26]

The printing work began by the new machine both in Odia and English language. After the starting of the press work, Fakir Mohan did not only save himself from shame, but his importance began to increase. From the first day of the press work, the people of Balasore came to see it. The press was named as "Fakir Mohan Senapati and Co- Utkal Press". Rich and poor men from far and near came in carts and palanquins to see its working. In the same manner as people had come in England to see Stephenson's first Railways, Fakir Mohan himself wrote in his autobiography . Like people streaming to a place of pilgrimage to see the car festival, crowds of curious men and women thronged to our press continuously for two to three months to see the working of the machine. Even rural zamindars came to Balasore in palanquins to see the wonder. Radhanath Roy told Fakir Mohan in an inaugural meeting at Madan Mohan's residence Zamindar of Balasore. The way you have set up the press will be recorded in letters of gold in the history of Odisha. [27]

After six months of the starting of the press, John Beams, the then collector and T.E. Ravenshaw, the great benefactor of Odisha jointly paid a visit to the press and gave a rupees, that amount was deposited in the Printing Company's account in the shape of two shares and returned to them with an amount of thirty rupees when the company was liquidated.

Fakir Mohan decided to publish a literary magazine for the spread and development of Odia literature in Odisha. The periodicals which existed earlier to the famine of 1866 included 'Jananruna', Arunnodaya' and Prabodha Chandrika. These were the mouth-piece of the Christian missionaries. Prior to this, Gourishankar Roy founded "Utkal Dipika ". So the Board of Directors of the printing company decided in favour of bringing out a journal on fortnightly basis. Accordingly a new magazine named 'Bodhadayini and Balasore Sambad Bahika were published in July 1868. The first part Bodhadayini included the literary works and the second part Sambad Bahika included the news items . First it was published as a monthly from July 1868 and after three years it became a weekly magazine from June 1871, From July 1868 to June 1871 Fakir Mohan was its editor. [28]

The publications of Bodhadayini and Balasore Sambad Bahika in 1868 by the endeavours of Fakir Mohan Senapati was the first way to a keen cultural craving. From june 1872, the name of this journal changed to Balasore Sambad Bahika. But its publication was stopped from 16 October 1873 to July 1874. It was published again from 1st August 1874. [29]

The British occupation of Odisha in 1803 wiped out the land from the political map of India by amalgamating it in parts with the adjoining provinces. As a result the people of other regions dominated, exploited and influenced the Odias and the cultural identity of Odia people was shattered. In the midst of the political and economic oppression of culture heritage of Odisha, he started his writings in " Sambad Bahika" not only for the upliftment of the Odias but for the challenge to Bengali language.

During the time of Fakir Mohan, it was found that there was a linguistic mixture of Odia language with Bengali. So it was regarded as Sankar (hybrid) language. Thus the educated Odias used to speak and write in Sankar language. Further improvement of mother tongue, Fakir Mohan wrote: " We appeal to cultured citizens that you should give up Sankar language by expressing your love and affection for your mother tongue. Whenever he caught sight of any onslaught on or negligence of the language , he used his pen in this context like a dauntless editor. Having seen the miserable condition of Odia language in the institutions run by the Bengali, he wrote in the Sambad Bahika citing the example of Barabati school of Balasore. [30]

In Sambad Bahika, many a discourse used to come out. Whenever Fakir Mohan found a new book, he would not waver to give his remark. With the publication of Odisha Itihas by Pyarimaohan Acharya in 1880 , Fakir Mohan remarked: "we have been pleased with the book cited above by going through the pros and cons about it. So long whatever text books have been composed in Odia language , most of them are versions . The number of original books are very few. Again among those few books, the number of really useful books is less. In this case, there is no doubt that we shall welcome a truly useful original book whenever we find it". [31]

Fakir Mohan strived tirelessly through the Sambad Bahika for the spread of education in Odisha. The Normal School was set up at Balasore in October 1873. The School had no permanent building. The british

Government sanctioned money for the construction of the building. But the Director of Education could not give its sanction order. SO Fakir Mohan appealed to the government through the Bahika for the construction of the building. [32]

Fakir Mohan realized that for the improvement of higher education in Odisha, it was necessary to increase the number of schools. He wrote for higher education in Odisha. There was necessity of opening other two schools. There was no doubt that an amount of twenty rupees can be spent. Then Bhadrak school can be also converted to a school of higher education.[33] "As a result of his demand, in January 1876 a college was established at Cuttack. But no fund was made to the development of the college. As the teachers were low paid, sincere teaching was not imparted to the students. In consequence the results of the students were not up to expectation. So with a view to removing these faults and flaws, Fakir Mohan wrote in Sambad Bahika :"had the Principal and lecturers received their full salary like those in other colleges, they would have been blamed for the bad result of the college. Hence whose was the fault? It was clear from simple reasoning that the fault was not with the students and teachers. It lies with the government." [34]

For the education in the Gujarat territories he wrote. "So long as the schools are not set up in Gujarat territories, there will be no development of this country. Because seventy five per cent of Odisha belongs to Gujarat territories and only twenty five per cent of it belongs to Moghalbandi." [35]

Fakir Mohan's writing was not opposed to modernization. But he cautioned us by way of exposing its bad effects. How best we could profit from it without corrupting and upsetting our tradition and value system, the article "Narijatira Paridheya Paribartan" or change of dress of womanhood was written by Fakir Mohan in the Sambad Bahika. In the article, he mooted the proposal for the women to use a dress Samejee to protect them from cold and to protect their modesty. [36]

By the second half of the 19th century there prevailed corruption and exploitation in Odisha society which shocked Fakir Mohan much . Through his writing he waged a constant war on the exploiters of society and exposed the weakness that was corroding the vital life forces of mankind. [37]

The journal Bodhadayini was at first managed by Fakir Mohan Senapati. But in October 1871, he was compelled to hand over its entire charge to Gobinda Chandra Pattanaik, Headmaster , Balasore Normal School when Fakir Mohan left for Nilgiri estate on his appointment to the post of Dewan. [38]

4.7 FAKIR MOHAN AS A SOCIAL REFORMER

The 19th century was a period of social reformation in Odisha. There prevailed superstition and blind beliefs in Odisha society. The society was dominated by ancient bad customs. Education was not widespread and there was the fear of robbers. The society was dominated by the crooked saints and monks. Semi-educated persons took delight in pride and vanity. They were ready to sip water from the drain in the name of civilization deriding all ancient traditional values. [39]

Fakir Mohan wanted the reformation of the society through his writings. In the writings of Fakir Mohan this reformative irony expressed itself. His novels and short stories were written with a view to reforming many aspects of the society. Fakir Mohan had declared war on the prevailing bad customs and anti-social elements through his stories. The specialty of his stories was to pass a scathing remark in tongue –in-the-cheek manner against immorality and justice of the contemporary society. [40]

Fakir Mohan was mainly a social reformer. He was not writing for writing's sake. So he wanted to organize people's opinion and rouse their consciousness through this satire against various bad customs of the society. Fakir Mohan proved himself a great social critic and reformer in most of his novels. As a great satirist he relentlessly exposed social maladies which were the offshoot of western civilization. [41]

The female society of Odisha was in a state of negligence. They had no liberty. The gate of education was closed for them, the system of 'kanyasuna' remained in the society; the widows were not permitted to remarry and had to live an unbearable life. So Fakir Mohan wanted to end the seclusion of women in the society. In most of his short stories he pointed out the emancipation of woman. On the activities of woman, Khageswar Mohapatra wrote:"the role of woman in the society is strong and influential. Woman is the life-centre of the society. She is an adoring idol. A sense of discipline of the society. It is an important duty of the society to keep up the prestige of woman and on the other hand the duty of woman is to maintain discipline in the society. Exception in the activities of man is tolerable and it is naturally accepted. But the slightest exception of woman disturbs the discipline of the society. Those women who are neglected, fallen and blamed in the society for different reasons, their reaction reflects on society. It creates indiscipline in the society.[42] There were female characters in Fakir Mohan's writing who were responsible for the peace of the society. The characters like Marua, Manika, Ghalahi, Nakaphodiama etc. were widows. They were the poison of the society. Being deprived of conjugal bliss these women derived a sadistic pleasure out of causing harm to others. For the organization of the society, arrangements should be made for these women. On this matter, different thoughts of Fakir Mohan had been published in his writings like Bidhaba Chandrapravara Nirjala Akadasi, Ramrath, Barabilasini and Bidhabara Avisapa.

Towards the last part of the 19th century, most of the social reforms raised voice for widow remarriage and female education. It was due to the effort of Iswar Chandra Vidyasagar that the government permitted widow remarriage in 1856. This revolutionary thought influenced the reformers of Odisha which was seen in the works of Fakir Mohan. narrating the role of a widow in society, her nature and deformity in his novels and short stories. Fakir Mohan had not only warned the Odia society, but also declared in powerful language his support to introduction of as a principal duty among various measures of progress in his poem ' Bidhabara Avisapa', a pen picture of the semester aspect of widow practice was presented .[43]

In Fakir Mohan's novel 'Chhaman Attaguntha',the female character Champa was a cruel and treacherous lady. She could only be compared with Shakespere's Lady Macbeth, Chitrakala the female Character in the novel 'Mamu' was a terrible intelligent. Terribly corrupt call-girl, Tara Dei in Fakir Mohan's novel 'Prayaschitta' was like Champa and Chitrakala. These types of characters were the seeds of the poison that poisoned the whole being of the society . Fakir Mohan wanted to make the society free from their strong grasp.[44]

Fakir Mohan was in favour of female education. The daughter of Fakir Mohan, Sarojini was the first school educated lady in Balasore. He also wrote in his autobiography that for the spread of female education in Balaore he got sufficient help from John Beams, the collector of Balasore . The chief aim of most of his stories was the introduction of female education . He wrote: "Only Christian girl students were reading in Mission Girl's School. Fakir Mohan goes and sits in the school in order to listen to the reading of books, recitation of poems by the girls. He not only gets delighted but also becomes hopeful about the education of the Hindu maidens.[45] But the affair was impossible, because at that time female education was impracticable in Hindu society. It was believed that if a girl took her lesson, she would be a widow, vegetables never got boiled in the prepared curry, and the curry became unsavory without salt. But Fakir Mohan who had done his work like a hero in all other fields, did not lag behind in this contact and had set up the girls school at Balasore,

The story "Rebati" is the finest example of Fakir Mohan's thought on female education. In this story there was a struggle between the ancient society which opposed female education and the spread of female education . But in spite of opposition by the old society. Rebati, a fine female character of the story, started her education. The superstitions and bad customs which had been gathered in the simple hearts of the country folk conventionally for ages, although found an expression in the character or Rebatis's grandmother , had gradually become feeble and expressed itself through universal affection and grace . In the story " Pathoi Babu", due to lack of education, the uneducated wife of Gopal Chandra Pattanaik could not understand the meaning of "Bhaktidayini Sabha" which meant to her " Bhagabati Dahani" Latter on she understood it. [46]

Fakir Mohan had also realized that the women could not use the proper dresses owing to want of education . In some place , he wrote that the Hindu women could not come out in dress covering their chest. For want of education , they were falling a prey to the wicked men. [47]

The main aim of his stories was to reform the society. To achieve this goal, humour was accepted as a principal medium, to reform the society through satirical works was his chief purpose. Fakir Mohan was a supporter of liberty of women which was seen in his story " Garudi Mantra"

Fakir Mohan pointed out the social evils like the selling of the girls in the story " Birai Bisal' and Madhamahantika Kanyasuna'. There prevailed in the society the evil of marriage of young girls to aged persons by giving money to the father of the girls. Fakir Mohan described the consequences of such marriages in his stories. [48]

The story 'Sona Bahu' is the finest example of Fakir Mohan's concern for the womanhood. He wanted that there should be hundreds of superstition – free ' Sona Bahu' in each and every house of Odisha. The idealism of female character was obvious in various ways through the characters of Satnami and Saria of 'Chhaman Athaguntha', Haripriya Devi and Indumati of Prayaschitta', Menaka Dei and Saraswati Dei of ' Mammu', the Maharani of Raibanigarh and Lachhama of ' Lachhama', Rebati,

Sulochana Devi , wife of Kubera Sahu , Padmabati Chemi etc, of Galpasalpa , remaining within the discipline of the society as mother , sister, lover , daughter and a life–mate these characters always tried to keep up the prestige of each other . It was healthy and disciplined society by removing some common follies of character like want of education, superstition, religious faith, too much simplicity and other inclinations to superstition. [49]

Fakir Mohan pointed out in 'Chhaman Athaguntha', 'Mauna mauni', and 'Dhulia Baba' how the society had deteriorated in the name of religion. How the saints committed hypocrisy and assault in the name of religion was found in these great works. He tried to save the society from the influence of these monks by exposing their true nature.

Fakir Mohan wanted to save the society from the exploitations of landlords. Therefore he exposed the nature of the landlords and to save the society he tried to make the people conscious through his novels and short stories. Due to the sun-set laws of the British government, a new class of zamindars arose in place of traditional zamindars. Their justified representative was Rama Chandra Mangaraj of 'Chhaman Athaguntha', who was an exploitative nature of the zamindar. In his work 'Rebati', 'Savya Zamindar', and Adharma Bitta, [50] the social superstitions were exposed by him.

As a social reformer, his specialty was not to bring about a thorough change all of a sudden like the extremists. He wanted little change in the society according to time. He was hesitant to launch forth a destructive reformation in the manner if ' Kalapahad', by shattering the stereotyped society. Its main cause was his profound love and respect for Odia society and the Hindu traditional culture. [51]

With the immediate reformation of the society, what would be the result is described in Fakir Mohan's 'Patent Medicine', Savya Zamindar', and 'Dakmunsi' with immediate introduction of Western education and civilization. In Patent Medicine', Chandramani's life deteriorated through lechery and debauchery. The rapid introduction of English education, in 'Dakmunsi, the son misbehaved and used Enlgish Bhusi to his father. Due to this rapid modernization of the women society, women failed to give respect to superiors , and the story ' Savya Zamindar ' is the finest example where the society could not welcome the modern educated lady.

Having learnt English the educated youth were anxious to enter the services, and by learning Western educational manners and principles. They always preferred to speak English and started condemning their parents and superiors and the customs relating to the tradition of this country. So Fakir Mohan made efforts to make the contemporary society developed and beatified not by fragmenting it, but by removing all its stigma and filthiness. In the true sense of the term, Fakir Mohan was a reformer. It was his intensions to make the society cultured and refined on the pedestal of Conservation. It was Fakir Mohan's ideology of social reformation not to give up those in society on which tradition was founded, but to regulate the society by them , exchanging a little or refining that tradition according to the situation . Fakir Mohan wanted a society not like the Bengali's. He wanted a pure Odia society. [52]

4.8 FAKIR MOHAN AS AN ADMINISTRATOR

Fakir Mohan Senapati was a diplomatic administrator. The diplomacy which he played during his service in the Tributary States of Odisha. Established peace and tranquility in those states by suppressing the popular rising, the blood of Khatriya dynasty which was in his veins from his great grandfather, Hanu Mallah, crated him as a strong administrator The word ' Khandayat' was justified for him both meanings of king and administrator. As an administrator in the Tributary States of Odisha, he showed remarkable skill, Intelligence, shrewdness and sagacity. From 1871 to 1896 he held the charge of administration of Nilgiri, Dompara, Dhenkanal, Daspalla, Palalahara and Keonjhar. Wherever he was, Senapati made a mark as an administrator also, cleverly tackling many a knotty problem of revenue administration. Inter-state disputes, personal problems of the chiefs, even quelling revolts and rebellions.

John Beams getting well acquainted with Fakir Mohan's calibre insisted him to be the "Dewan" of Nilagiri. He served as the Diwan of Nilagiri from 1871 to 1875 at a monthly salary of Rs.1, 000/- after which he served as "Diwan" at various places of Odisha. He was Diwan at Damapada from 1876 to 1877, at Dhenkanal from 1877 to 1883, at Daspalla from 1884 to 1886, at Pallahada from 1886 to 1887, at Keonjhar from 1887 to 1892, at Damapada for the second time from 1894 to 1896. He stayed at Cuttack from 1896 to 1905 and was attached with various institutions of literature. He spent his last time at Balasore till death.

Though Fakir Mohan was a semi-educated man with a schooling of two and a half years, the good relation that he had established with the British officials placed him as the Dewan of several Tributary States of Odisha. On the recommendation of John Beams, the collector of Balasore, Fakir Mohan was appointed as the Dewan of Nilgiri state in Balasore District at the age of twenty-nine by the Superintendent of Tributary States with the monthly salary of One hundred rupees. He had no experience regarding the administration. But he knew that the welfare of the governed was the duty of the ruler. With this motto, some development works were undertaken by him. The construction of a road from Nilgiri to Sergarh and establishment of a Market in the name of queen ' Nirmala' were two great works of Fakir Mohan. It paved the way for trade and commerce. He introduced the cultivation of cabbage and peas. He also took steps of Nilgiri. For the spread of Sanskrit education among the Brahmins, steps were taken by him to establish Sanskrit tolls. As the Brahmins were ignorant and did not know the merit of education, they disagreed on the proposal of Fakir Mohan. On the other hand, they went against him. He had been criticized as a cruel administrator, when he made plans to increase the tax on the cutting of stones . So he resigned form his post. [53]

In Dompara and Keonjhar, his activities, courage, prestige, skill and inventiveness could be proved. On taking the charge of Dewanship of Dompara. Fakir Mohan found a continuation of uprising. The Subjects used to send allegations to the magistrate against the king. In these circumstances Fakir Mohan had taken over the charge. Before Fakir Mohan's taking charge there, John Beams the Collector of Cuttack had advised him, "at least for three months you will remain silent and do not do anything. For five years there has been disturbances between the king and the subjects , News are reaching about various litigations . You will see as if the disturbance would not rise, it is only your duty".[54]

But on the arrival of the new Dewan on behalf of the government, instead of being calmed down the great uprising of Dompara thickened fast. Fakir Mohan saw that the royal family was in face of great disaster owing to the non-cooperation of the subjects. It was declared by the leaders of the rising that nobody would go to Raja's palace , nobody would work there and even the washer man and barber would not work for the king. As a result the clothes of the women in palace were washed at Cuttack.

The Raja Raghunath Mansingh, Banambar Roy was an obstinate ruler. The Raja was not ready to accept any proposal of Fakir Mohan. The main cause of the uprising was that, the Raja wanted to make fresh settlement of the land to fix the land revenue on the basis of its area. After the death of Purusottom Mansingh, Banambar Roy, the British government selected Raghunath Manshing , son of the brother of Purusattom Mansing, as the successor, but Raghunath was a minor at the time of the death of Purutsottam. So the state came under the court of wards. During that period the land revenue settlement was done by the manager of the state and revenue was fixed on a relaxed basis and the subjects enjoyed rent-fee arable land. When Raghunath Mansing took charge of the state, he wanted to make new subjects and decided not to give more revenue. For this reason the conflict started between the Raja and his subjects. As a result, the rising began and the leader of the rising was Nidhi Pattanaik, ex-dewan of the king.

Fakir Mohan discussed with the leaders of the rising to solve this, but it failed at the policy which he adopted brought him success. The way in which the British government could be handicapped and paralised, non-cooperation movement launched by Gandhiji in the same way Fakir Mohan came with the banner of success foiling the rising of Dompara. [55]

To make the last compromise John Beams the collector of Cuttack paid a visit to Dompara with Police Superintendent, one Assistant Magistrate, twenty constables, Pescara, munsi, amalas and chaparasis. On the arrival of the Collector, Fakir Mohan described all the facts of the resin. He narrated that it was created by the Padhans and the Amalas. The rent-fee land was not enjoyed by the subjects father, the rent was collected by the Padhanas and Amalas from the people and that amount was being utilized by them.

The administration in Keonjhar was a remarkable chapter in Fakir Mohan's life during his manage at Keonjhar, once he even gave up the hope of remaining alive for the Bhuyan rising. On his arrival at Anandapur firstly, he made good arrangement of the official record in the success of a case in favour of Keonjhar state. He won the confidence of the king Dhananjaya Narayan Bhanja and his monthly salary increased to one hundred twenty rupees from june 1889. The most important achievement of Fakir Mohan was the establishment of a press at Anandapur, reformation of the kacheri house and the lifting of an unjust tax introduced at Anandapur. [56]

Fakir Mohan proved himself an intelligent and clever administrator by suppressing the Bhuyan rebellion of Keonjhar. The Bhuyans were an ancient tribe peculiar to the state.

Rose in rebellion in 1891, the leader of the rising was Dharanidhar who was educated at Cuttack survey School at the expenses of Maharaja of Keonjhar and then employed under the king of Keonjhar state. The Cause of the rising was waterfall named 'Machakandaana at Joda. For the purpose of cultivation, manager Fakir Mohan planned to divert hot water of the fall rapiers eastern side. Accordingly the construction of a canal started and it was place in charge of Bhichitrananda Das. Assistant Manager of Keonjhar state. The work was done by the Bhuyans without wage. Even they brought their day meals and worked from morning to evening. For the negligence of the work they were beaten. Owing to hard work they rose in rebellion .

About the cause of the rising Pandit Mrutunjay Rath wrote in 'Utkal Sahitya' that Maharaja Dhanajaya Bhanj was an oppressive ruler . The subjects specially the Bhuyans rose in revolt against his oppression and Dharanidhar, a Bhuyan youth became its leader. He was educated at Cuttack survey School at the royal expense and worked as an honorary surveyor. In the boundary dispute of Keonjhar and Singhbhum, Dharani was sent to the place of dispute by the king. There he was informed that his brother and some other Bhuyans were imprisoned by the orders of the king and he should get the same on his arrival. As a result Dharani gave up royal work and took shelter at his brother-in-law Narendra Mohapatra's house . To remove the oppression he collected funds from the Bhuyans. In 1891, the Bhuyans sent a petition to the Commissioner and a copy to the Manager of Mayurbhanj. when no step was taken the Bhuyans assembled before him and with them he started plundering for their livelihood. [57]

During his service at different places, Fakir Mohan was much esteemed by the people for his beneficial work. Fakir Mohan dam, Fakir Mohan Dungi, and the construction of a road in Daspalla. Fakir Mohan Bungalow and Krushnapriya well in Dompara and Machakandana Joda or irrigation project in Keonjhar were some of the examples of his work. Wherever Fakir Mohan remained in his life-time. There he started reformative works and new plans like education, use of administrative offers, Trade and commerce, Communication, Irrigation and water facilities.

In his new Dewani life as a part and parcel of administrative endeavor , the misdeeds which he had done and which he should not have confessed the regretful confession that he had left for others, proved his extraordinarily natural purity of his personality always reminded us of the German literary creator , Goethe as a dewan of Wymer , a small German feudal state . Had

Fakir Mohan spent his administrative life time like Goethe in one state , we would have seen an established ideal state under his guidance. [58]

4.9 POVERTY

There is an amusing story of how his family came to close their property. When the Honorable East India Company occupied Odisha in 1803, his grandmother, Kuchila Dei, was a young widow with two small sons, one or two years old and another four.

According to Granny, the Company troops approached Balasore from both south and east. The moment they reached Balaramgarh , at the river-mouth east of Balasore, the villagers fled for their lives , leaving all their possessions and taking with them into the forests only their relations. Peace was shortly established. Assured by the Company that no harm would come to them. The villagers returned home. Lots of them had fled in such terror that they had not even stopped to shut their doors. On their return they found their backyards loaded with ripe fruit, for everyone had been so afraid for his life, that no one had time to think of stealing.

After some months the East India Company had established its good government in Odisha, it was proclaimed that people were to be allowed to retain the property and possessions they had enjoyed under the Marathas. All that was required in property owner should present themselves at the government office on a pre-determined date and registered their deed with the collector. Most of the owner failed to turn up, either because of fear or to understand the government proclamation. So foot soldiers with warrants were sent to escort them there. One day, one comes to the house of Fakir Mohan Senapati. Fakir Mohan's granny was then a young widow. Granny lay her two boys in a corner, covered them with a mat and called through a crack in the door: "We have no male children in this house. We have no need of land". The villagers backed her up, so the soldiers went off and Fakir Mohan's family lost their land and became poor. [59]

The views of the Odia critics on the economic condition of Fakir Mohan Senapati lack unanimity. Some described him as extremely poor where as others attempted to justify his sound economic condition. Fakir Mohan Senapati's contemporary Odia luminaries like Radhanath Rai, Nandakishor Bala and Brajamohan Panda described Fakir Mohan as a poverty-stricken man.[60]

Fakir Mohan himself acknowledged his poverty and family burden in his brief autobiography. Fakir Mohan stated that he had to complete his School education without having a shirt to wear due to poor economic condition of his father. Poverty compelled Fakir Mohan Senapati to engage himself in foot-soldiers.

However, there is no two opinions about the fact that Fakir Mohan Senapati had to undergo economic hardship during the formative years of his life. Through poverty and lack of communication were two major stumbling blocks in his getting exposure to western education, Fakir Mohan Senapati emerged victorious in the test of life and proved his credibility as a great educationist. What is more important is not his poverty, but the defeat of poverty in his life.

4.10 CHARACTER

Though Fakir Mohan spent most part of his life working under the Zamidar, he never compromised with his self-respect, truthfulness, honesty and dignity.

Fakir Mohan believed in simple living and high thinking. He never aspired for material prosperity. He was satisfied with what he was.

Fakir Mohan wore not just a gentle and innocent look, but in reality he was gentle from the core of his heart. He was imbibed with all the moral virtues like honesty, fraud and unfair means, and never wished to become a part of any conflict or dispute. He cherished not only a moral character but a spiritual as well. He engaged himself in devotional activities from his very beginning. His spiritualistic frame of mind found expression in many of his literary creations.

Fakir Mohan Senapati was so honest that he did not hesitate to appear as a witness in a case field against his employer, the Zamindar of different places as well as teacher.

Fakir Mohan was a social-reformer too. It was during the last phase of his life. After his retirement from service, he worked to bring some reforms in the traditions and practices of his own community.

Fakir Mohan was a man of emotion. At the time of any discussion he discussed emotionally the good side of the topic. Many times we had seen him crying like a boy in his worship.

Fakir Mohan had love and affection for all. He never found fault with anybody. His heart was like a 'Rasgola' in it there were two juices adequately mixed. It was not know whether anger took its place in his mind. He did not do any harm to anybody. Whatever harm anybody had committed he was not making haste to take revenge. His quality of forgiveness was admirable.[61]

Fakir Mohan was a religious man. In every moment of work he took the name of God. In childhood he worshipped 'Siva' and took to fasting on Monday. But later on he was converted to Brahma religion and founded Brahma Samaj at Balasore.

Fakir Mohan believed in 'Karma' or deeds. Even at the last stage of life. He never stopped his work. He did not neglect to make correspondence with his friends even in his state of tiredness. He advised the youth for the right action and was ready to join in every right institution. At the last stage of his life, he presided over the 13th session of Utkal Sammilani Conference and he delivered his final advice taking up the post of president of Utkal Students Conference.

Fakir Mohan was very much fond of students. He looked upon them affectionately as they were the future of the country. He had a strong memory. He could remember the years, months, and days of many events. For that many used in shipping trade in those days were found in his stories.

It was a result of his sharp memory. Many ancient reports of great families of Orissa were known to him. He was justly the old grandfather of the educated public in telling the ancient tales of the country.

The best quality if Fakir Mohan's life was his love for garden. At Cuttack residence, he had a small garden having plants of many flowers and fruits. Beating plants he watered them with his own hands. He had set up his another residence at Mallikashpur and named it as 'Shantikanan',. Having spent the last period of his life in that 'Shantikanan', he left for his heavenly abode from there.

Fakir Mohan Senapati was a poetic genius, a prolific writer, an educationist, a philosopher, a social reformer and a nationalist. After leading a complete life this multifaceted personality breathed his last on 14th June 1918 at the age of seventy five.

REFERENCES

1. John Boulton, Atma Jivana Carita of Fakir Mohan Senapati, 1995, Orissa Sahitya Akademi, P4.
2. Ibid,P.2
3. Ibid,P.1
4. Ibid,PP.4-5
5. Fakir Mohan Senapati, Autobiography,(Oriya),1981, Cuttack P-4
6. B.K. Satpathy (ed), Fakir Mohan His Life and literature,1984, Balasore,P.2
7. Fakir Mohan Senapati .op.cit p.6
8. Golak Chandra Mohapatra, Senapati Fakir Mohan (Oriya), 1986, Balasore .p.5
9. B.K.Satpathy (ed.), op.cit pp.36-37
10. Fakir Mohan Senapati , op.cit .pp.5.6
11. Ibid p.16
12. Mayadhar Mansingh, Saraswati Fakir Mohan (Oriya) ,1981 Cuttack p.29.
13. Ibid.p.31
14. Ibid.p.32
15. Fakir Mohan Senapati .op.cit.pp.23-25
16. Ibid.p.26
17. B.K Sathpathy(ed),op.cit.P.6
18. Fakir Mohan Senapati, op.cit. p. 26
19. Ibid.p.27
20. Report in General Administrative of Orissa Division 1872.1873 Para9

21. Sarbeswar Das, Jugasrasta Fakir Mohan(Oriya), 1983, Berhampur, P.16

22. Mayadhar Mansingh, op.cit.p 14

23. Fakir Mohan Senapati, op.cit.p.14

24. Ibid,p.15

25. Mayadhar Mansingh, op.cit..p 40

26. B. K Satpathy(ed),op.cit.p.38

27. Fakir Mohan Senapati, op.cit.p.40

28. Sambad Bahika,1 August 1874

29. P. C. Mohanty (ed), Senapati Sahityaloka (Oriya),1989 Balasore, p .174

30. Sambad Bahika 1 Ocotober 1874

31. Ibid. 19 February 1880

32. P.C. Mohanty (ed), .op.cit.p. 180

33. Sambad Bahika, 22 November 1877.

34. Ibid 7 January 1878

35. Ibid. 1 January 1875

36. Srinibas Mishra, Adhunika Oriya Gadhaya Sahitya (Oriya) 1978 Cuttack P.141

37. K.C. Jena, The Ascendancy of the British Raj in Orissa . 1982 Calcutta p.120.

38. Natabar Samantaray Vyasabi Fakir Mohan (Oriyas) . 1957 Cuttack pp. 48-49

39. Braja Mohan Mohanty, Adhunika Oriya Sahitya (Oriya) 1963 Cuttack, p. 62

40. Surendra Mohanty, Oriya Sahityara Kramabisaka (Oriya), 1963 Cuttack p.62.

41. M.N. Das (ed), Side Lights on History and Culture of Orissa. 1977, Cuttack p. 718.

42. Khageswar Mohapatra,Fakir Mohan O Oriya Samaj Jhankar (Oriya,Part XVI. 11th Number 1965 Cuttack,pp.1012-1013

43. Ibid,pp. 1013-1014

44. Surendra Mohanty, Fakir Mohan Samikshya (Oriya) 1972 . Cuttack p. 42

45. Srinibas Mishra , Adhunika Oriya Gadhya Sahitya (Oriya) 1978 Cuttack p. 153.

46. B.C. Samal, Oriya Galpa Srasta Manas Part 1 (Oriya), 1978 Cuttack pp 7-8.

47. Golak Chandra Mohapatra, op.cit.p.41

48. B.C . Samal ,op.cit.pp.18.20

49. Khageswar Mohapatra, op.cit.pp.1013-1014

50. B.C.Acharya, Oriya Sahityara Sankhipta Parichaya (Oriya). 1977. Cuttack p.208

51. Khageswar Mohapatra, op.cit. p.1015

52. Surendra Mohanty, Fakir Mohan Samikshya (Oriya) , 1972 Cuttack pp. 21-22.

53. Fakir Mohan Senapati, op.cit .p 51

54. Ibid p. 58

55. Mayadhar Mansingh . op. cit.. pp .94-95.

56. Prafulla Chandra Mohanty,Fakir Mohan Sahityare Samakalina Orissa Chitra (Oriya).1984. Cuttack.p.112.

57. Fakir Mohan Senapati ,op.cit.pp.102.104.
58. Mayadhar Mansingh,op.cit.pp..91-92.
59. John Boulton, Atma Jivana Carita of Fakir Mohan Senapati, 1995, Orissa Sahitya Akademi, PP.1-2.
60. D.K.Dash, Gangadhar: Kavita O Kavi-atma, Rourkela: Pragati Utkal Sangha, 1995,P.179.
61. Chandra Mohan Moharana, Fakir Mohan Utkala Sahitya(Oriya), Part 22, 4th number, Srabana,P.192.

♦♦♦

CHAPTER-V

LITERARY WORKS OF FAKIR MOHAN SENAPATI

CHAPTER V

LITERARY WORK OF FAKIR MOHAN SENAPATI

"When there is the bustle of progress everywhere, will Utkal be still in slumber?" This line from Fakir Mohan's first original poem *Utkal Bhraman* (Tours of Orissa) not only epitomises his literary overview but also depicts his flare for Odia nationalism. Fakir Mohan Senapati, regarded as the father of modern Odia literature, dedicated his entire life for the progress of Odia language. He also played a leading role in establishing the distinct identity of Odia language and literature. So the story of Fakir Mohan is indeed the story of the "renaissance" in Odia literature.

Unlike his predecessors, Fakir Mohan completely discarded the traditional theme of romantic love between prince-princess and wrote about common people and their problems in his novels. In contrast to the Sanskritised style of his contemporaries, he also used colloquial idiomatic Odia in his writings with great skill and competence. If the works of earlier novelists seemed like prose renderings of medieval *kavyas*, Fakir Mohan's novels were realistic to the core. Fakir Mohan can be favorably compared with twentieth century novelists like Premchand and Bibhutibhusan Banerjee.[1]

Fakir Mohan lived and wrote during the darkest period of Odishan history. Odias then had no state of their own and lived scattered in three neighbouring states i.e. Bengal, Central Provinces and Madras. Odias had little opportunity to develop their literature and culture. On the other hand, there was the onslaught on Odia language from the neighboring states like Bengal and the Telugu of Vizagpatnam Agency. British bureaucrats of the Central Provinces tried to hurt the feelings of the Odias which resulted in historic language agitation in the respective areas. Though all the three agitations were aimed at unification of Odia speaking regions, the root cause of each agitation was different from each other. This "*Desha Mishran*

Andolan" or the movement to bring all the Odia speaking areas under one political administration took place during Fakir Mohan's time. It was felt that if Odia language was to survive, then it was important to enrich the modern Odia literature along with text books. In this backdrop Fakir Mohan began his literary career as a writer of text books. His writing of text books was prompted by his zeal of opposing the move to abolish Odia from schools of Odisha. That is why, Odia nationalism was a dominant theme in Odia literature during late nineteenth and early twentieth centuries.

Fakir Mohan is considered as the greatest prose writer in Odia literature. But it is amazing to note that he hardly wrote any prose until he retired from administrative service. He translated Ramayan, Mahabharat and some of the Upanishads from the original Sanskrit for which he is popularly known as *Vyasa Kavi*. He wrote poetry too, but the themes of his written were not considered conventionally fit material for prose. He used colloquial, spoken and rugged language of the common man which no written in Odia had done for centuries. Fakir Mohan wrote four novels, two volumes of short-stories and one autobiography. Besides that, he mastered the art of writing short stories for which he is also termed as *Katha Samrat* (Emperor of Shortstories) in Odia literature. [2]

He had absolutely no ambition to blossom out as a poet or a writer. He adopted literature as an experimental means. His extraordinary creative powers were revealed only as he went on writing miscellaneously. Fakir Mohan has enriched modern Odia literature through stories novels, poems and translations. His autobiography is regarded as the immortal treasure of Odia literature. His literature is rich with the portraits of unimportant and neglected characters drawn from the masses. He has satirized the old customs and superstitions of the past and has frowned upon the extrovert and unhappy civilized society of the present as well. [3]

In the last decade of 19th century some non-Odia officers tried their best to uproot Odia language from the government officers and the schools.

After the famine of 1866, T.E. Ravenshaw was determined to do all within his power to compensate the Odias for the loss in the Odias. Up to this time the Bengalis had influence over Odisha. They not only hated the Odias but also Biharis and occupied officers and schools, Brundaban Chandra Mandal was made the leader of the Bengalis.

Lachhama is a story of the Maratha invasion of Odisha which depicts the suffering and the heroic resistance of an Odia country girl in the face of invasion. "*Chha Mana Atha Guntha*" is a vivid account of the exploitation of poor village folk by *Zamindars. Mamu*, again is a story of exploitation of village folk by petty government officials and clerks "*Prayaschita*" potrays the predicament of a semi-educated youth who persistently defies the old order of things with an overenthusiasm for new western values.[4]

Exploitation of the poor villagers by *Zamindars* and the rise of a new class of exploiters among the petty officials and clerks under the British Government were the two dominant traits of nineteenth century Odisha's social history and Fakir Mohan chose to write about them in "*Chha Mana Atha Guntha* and *Mamu*. In this last novel he studied the conflict between traditional Indian values and western values as understood by the educated youth of the time, which clearly suggests that he was neither a traditionalist nor an over-zealous advocate for the new wave of westernization that was sweeping the country during his time.

Exploitation of the poor by the rich was a dominant theme in Indian fiction, especially in the Thirties and Forties. Fakir Mohan is perhaps the first Indian novelist to write about it, thus anticipating works like Premchand's "*Godan*". Though Fakir Mohan was almost a contemporary of the great Bengali novelist Bankim Chandra Chatterjee, he was surprisingly different from Chatterjee about the choice of theme as well as language and style. Fakir Mohan's colloquial style is in sharp contrast with Chatterjee's high flown Sanskritised prose.[5]

Fakir Mohan's sense of humour and irony has remained unsurpassed in Odia literature and it is his characteristic style which made him popular with a wide range of readers. He believed that Faith, Asceticism, Love and Devotion were four pillars that formed the base of '*Dharma*'. His faith was derived from Islam, asceticism from Buddhism, love from Christianity and devotion from Vaishnavism.

Table with regard to Values in Fakir Mohan's novels and short stories

Sl. No.	Name of the Novels	Year of Publication	Values
1	Chha Mana Atha Guntha	1897-1899 (Utkal Sahitya Patrika & as a Novel in 1902)	Educational, Social & Ethical value
2	Lachhama	1903	Educational, Social & Historical value
3	Mamu	1913	Educational, Social & Ethical value
4	Prayaschita	1915	Educational, Social & Ethical value

The stories of Fakir Mohan were published in the book Galpa Salpa'. The year of publication name of the magazine in which published and name of the story are as follows:-[6]

Sl. No.	Name of the Story	Name of magazine in which published	Month & Year of Publication	Values
1	Lachhamania	Bodhadayini	1868(not available)	------
2	Rebati	Utkal Sahitya 2nd part, 10th number	October 1898	Social & educational value
3	Mauna Mauni	Mukura, 2nd part 2nd number	May 1907	Ethical value
4	Baleswari Rahajani	Mukura, 2nd part 4th number	July 1907	Social & ethical value
5	Baleswari Panga Luna	Mukura, 2nd part 6th number	September 1907	Social value
6	Punar Musika Bhaba	Mukura, 4th part 1st & 2nd number	April, May 1909	Educational value

7	Daaka Munsi	Mukura, 7th part 6th number	September 1912	Social, Ethical & Educational value
8	Dhulia Baba	Utkal Sahitya 16th part, 11th number	February 1913	Social & Educational value
9	Kamala Prasad Goraap	Utkal Sahitya 17th part, 2nd number	May 1913	Educational value
10	Sunaa Bahu	Utkal Sahitya 17th part, 3rd number	June 1913	Educational & Social value
11	Raandipua Anantaa	Mukura, 8th part 4th number	July 1913	Social, Ethical & Educational value
12	Kaalika Prasad Gorap	Utkal Sahitya 17th part, 5th number	August 1913	Social & Ethical value
13	Patent Medicine	Utkal Sahitya 17th part, 6th number	September 1913	Social, Ethical & Educational value
14	Beerei Bishala	Utkal Sahitya 17th part, 7th number	October 1913	Social Education value
15	Sabhya Jamidar	Utkal Sahitya 17th part, 12th number	March 1914	Social & Ethical value
16	Bagala Baguli	Utkal Sahitya 18th part, 1st number	April 1914	Ethical & Educational value
17	Ajaa Nati Katha	Utkal Sahitya 19th part, 1st number	April 1915	Social & Educational value
18	Pathoi Bahu	Mukura, 10th part 3rd number	June 1915	Educational & Ethical value
19	Adharma Bitta	Utkal Sahitya 19th part, 5th number	August 1915	Social Educational value
20	Madha Mohantynka Kanya Suna	Utkal Sahitya 19th part, 7th number	October 1915	Social & Ethical value
21	Gaarudi Mantra	Utkal Sahitya 20th part, 8th number	November 1916	Social & Educational value

Beside the stories Fakir Mohan should have written other few stories. His story 'Kabitwa Bisarjan' was published in the guise of 'Shree ' in eleven volumes in the part first and second of 1st and 3rd number of 'Mukura' In the letter of Fakir Mohan to Biswanath Kar, editor of 'Utkal Sahitya' he wrote on 1 April 1917, Knowing your request I have started writing a story in the name of 'Bisamanji' In another letter to him on 27 June 1915, he wrote ; 'I saw that many Bengali magazines flourished for stories, For that I tried to write stories." The last stories were written in the last part of Fakir Mohan's life when he was in sick bed, probably not succeeded in producing so many masterpieces.[7]

Fakir Mohan was not the founder of Odia novel. His rise as an Odia novelist was spontaneous. Before Fakir Mohan, the novels 'Padmamali' of Umesh Chandra and Bibasini of Ramshankar were published. But Fakir Mohan's genius and artistic success gave novel a new foundation and dignity in Odia literature , For that if not from historical point of view. He is respected as the father of Odia novel. In Odia literature he is respected as a successful novelist.

But in Odia novel, Fakir Mohan was different from them. He gave a new spirit and vigour to Odia novels of his time. His novels were written on the hard and stark reality of the present day society . He introduced the problematic social novels instead of romantic and historical novels. It would not be an exaggeration to say that he ushered in an epoch-making era not only in Odia novel, but also in the growth of fiction of Indian novels.[8]

In European fiction the first part of 19th century was the golden age of historical novels. The prominent were Dumas and Victor Hugo of France when Bankinm Chandra started writing novels. The English novelist Charles Dicken's novels of character and society were a remarkable success. But Bankim Chandra was not influenced by Dickens rather more influenced by Walter Scott. Even the Urdu novelist wrote the historical novels in the style of Scott. This manner of novel writing. its purpose and background in the first half of 19th century were published in Umesh Chandra's Padmabati and Ramshankar's ' Bibasini' . The Italian novelist Alessandro Maznoni's historical novel Promessi Sposi, the Betrothed was influenced by walter scott.[94] Fakir Mohan might have learnt to write novels from Bankim Chandra. Bankim Chandra was interested in presenting a glorious Hindu past and working for Hindu regeneration. On the other hand Fakir Mohan was interested mainly in depicting the present and working for a national regeneration.[9]

By the second half of 19th century English novel had obtained a social purpose. Dicken's best novel Oliver Twist was published before the birth of Fakir Mohan. But Fakir Mohan was not well educated in English to read all these novels. He did not look up to English or other European models. He rather looked into his heart and wrote after studying the life around him at first hand. Yet in style and form Fakir Mohan seems to be close to Dickens more faithfully. [10]

Fakir Mohan wrote four novels, namely Chhamana Athaguntha, Lachhama, Mamu, and Prayaschitta. All these novels were written in the last phase of Fakir Mohan's life. Besides these, Fakir Mohan in a letter to Biswanath Kar, mentioned about the writing of a long story "Bisamanji' on the request of Nandakishore, he wrote to change the same story into a novel.[11]

The publication of Chhamana Athaguntha was a memorable event in the history of novels. Before Fakir Mohan, Perhaps no such cruel picture of exploitation and plunder was published in a heart touching manner in any Indian language and literature. When novel was published periodically in 'Utkal Sahitya" it made much fuss in the reader's society. The period of writing of 'Chhaman Athaguntha' was from October 1897 to 1899 and the event of its description was from 1801 to 1840. In this novel he has started a discussion on the relation between the capitalist and down luodden class before 1900. But Bankim Chandra, Sarat Chandra of Bengali literature and Prem Chand of Hindi literature started their efforts after 1900. So Fakir

Mohan could be regarded as epoch-making writer among all bringing a change to Indian folklore literature. [12]

The novel 'Chhaman Athaguntha' portrays a war between the two societies, the downtrodden class and the oppressive capitalist class, similarly on one side tradition based ancient civilization and on the other side, progressive modern civilization. Oppression on rural life exploitation, Clever betrayal of the fanatics in the name of religion and waste of stricken administration have been delineated in it. The rise of a new zamindar class is seen in this novel by driving out the traditional zamindar class with the use of sunset law of the British government. The two institutions police and adalat and how they spent time in luxury have been exposed.

The novel 'Mamu' is the best creation of Fakir Mohan. The identity which he had given at the outset of 'Chhamana Athaguntha' was full-fledged in 'Mamu' the renaissance. Which made glimpses after suppression and oppression of Odisha is vivid and clear in this novel. In this novel, he set to describe the disintegration of a traditional culture and society by keeping contact with the West.

The last novel of Fakir Mohan was 'Prayaschita'. He describes how the tradition-bound society was destroyed with the contact of western civilization. He was not a man belonging to the age of 'Lachhama' or Chhaman Athaguntha' But he belonged to the contemporary age of 'Mamu' and 'Prayhschitta. That is why it is said that Fakir Mohan has depicted a partial picture of his family life in the novel 'Prayaschitta'.[13]

Fakir Mohan was a master craftsman in modern prose literature. For creation of prose in Odia literature his life was the only suitable source. in the last part of 19th century there was the necessity of genuine Odisha to create pure prose literature. During the last thirty years of the past century the unbecoming campaign of non-oriya language that continued against Odia language, only a pure Odia was needed to obstruct its way . He was the only symbol of this necessity .Fakir Mohan wrote : " At that time the

English and Parsi educated Babus of the country felt it to be a humiliation to touch the Odia books or speak Odia correctly.[14] The society also did not accept prose literature. The people were incapable of reading prose. They were reading the parables like songs in high time. But when they read as song if there was so rhyming, they threw away the books. In this situation, Fakir Mohan first took steps for the writing of biography and history. Before him some prose books were published, but the language employed was imitative in nature.

Fakir Mohan's prose literature has been divided into two phase. The first phase stretched from the writing of Rajputrara Itihas' till the period 1870. During this period he wrote ' Bharatavarsara itihas' and translated the biography written by Iswar Chandra Vidyasagar. The second phase lasted from 1897 to 1918. During this period he wrote stories, Novels, essays and autobiography. But from 1870 to 1897 when in service he wrote poems and translated puranas. [15]

Besides novels and stories, He wrote a number of essays. So it would not be an exaggeration to regard Fakir Mohan as an essayist. These essays were published in 'Utkal Sahitya' and Mukura' at different times. The essays are as follows: Yogasastra and Prakruti are two philosophical essays, Nanaka Panji is a satirical essay. The essay Gotra is an anthropological writing. 'Sudera' and 'Bedadhikar' are reformative essays. Utkal Bhaskara Bhuta Bhavisyata' Kabi Gopal Krishna Pattnaik, Kabi Maikel Madhusudan, Meghananda Badha, Utkala Sahityara Prana Pratistara Pratibanda, translation of Bengali version of Meghaduta are literary criticisms. The two speeches of Fakir Mohan as president of Cuttack Alochana Sabha' and Utkal Sahitya Samaj are agents of prosperity of his prose literature. Srikhetrare Chaityanamahaprabhu' and Balasore Bandharare Olandhaz Jati are two historical essays. Waltier Darshan is an adventurous writing. [16]

Fakir Mohan had also made substantial contribution to poetry in modern Odia literature. His first poem 'Utkal Bhraman' appeared in 1892.

Other poems of Fakir Mohan are Puspamala, Upahara, Abasarabasare, Pujaphoola, Prathana and Dhuli. He wrote a Kavya named 'Bhudhavatara Kavya'.[17]

The lyrics of Fakir Mohan were the outcome of deep sorrow and uncountable suffering. The early demise of his wife and the eldest child made him disconsolate at an old age. This misery and suffering finds an expression in the collection of his poems like Puspamala, Upahara, Pujaphoola. The dedicatory piece to 'Puspamala' kindles noble passions in the hearts of true lovers anywhere in the world. [18]

Fakir Mohan was a good translator. In 1866, he translated for the first time the biography written by Iswar Chandra Vidyasagar. This book was prescribed as the text book for the scholarship Examination only to beguile the melancholy hours of his wife, Krushna Kumari, after the death of their eldest child. He translated 'Ramayana and Mahabharat' single handed from Sanskrit to Odia. These two epics in the simplicity of language appealed even to the unlettered. After the publication of Ayodhyakanda ', One critic wrote, therefore we request that all the lettered people of Odisha should possess a copy of it . If the educated youth make their wives lettered and give them a copy of it, they could read it themselves and could learn many essential things like righteousness, Principle of the social ethics, Devotion to elders and husbands. At the time of the translation. Fakir Mohan's wife Krushna Kumari was with him. So he used simple language which would be understood by her. Besides these epics, Fakir Mohan took his hand or the translation of Chhandogaya Upanisada Bhagabatagita and Harivamsa. [19]

The literary ideal and creative vision of Fakir Mohan was revolutionary and progressive. As he had acquainted with the day to day life of the common people. Varieties of characterization and natural language came to him naturally. He used the common folk language and characters in his literature. Therefore, Fakir Mohan, the real pioneer of mass literature in

Odisha, can rightly be called the "Vyasakabi" for raising the ordinary characters to epic stature. [20]

The rural & urban life of the Odias and the events of the British rule are described in the novel Mamu. The attraction of English education for the Odias as seen here is historically correct. The rise of middle educated class and their role are described in the novel Prayaschitta. It is the history of development of organizations in Odisha. Utkal Sammilani and Utkal Sahitya Samaj are the examples of it.

Some of the stories of Fakir Mohan indicate the history of Odisha. The disturbances of the monks and the police constables are described in the story Mauna Mauni . He gives the real picture of overseas trade of Odisha and the ruin of shipping trade in Kamala Prasad Gorap and Kalika Prasad Gorap . The ruin of salt industry of Balsore is hinted in Balasori Pangaluna and Punarmushikabhava . Fakir Mohan wrote in his autobiography. "In my childhood there was a great shipping trade at Balasore. Five to six hundred ships were sailing in the sea. Twelve-four-score of ships were engaged in the transportation of salt. He has made the government control responsible for the ruin of salt industry. By the invasion of the Portugal pirates how the overseas trade of Odisha declined is portrayed in his stories. [21]

The autobiography of Fakir Mohan is a political economical, social and cultural history of Odisha from the second half of 19th century to first 18 years of 20th century. The condition of Odisha from the British occupation of Odisha in 1803 to the end of the First World war in 1918 is manifested in his autobiography. All historical events like the ancient educational policy of contemporary agitation of the neighbours and the language agitation by the Odias, the famine of 1866 establishment of the printing press, introduction of Odia text books, publication of Odia journals and scripts . The gradual development of the social, political and cultural aspects of Odisha, the blind rule of tributary rules, popular rising etc are narrated in it.[22]

The Odia society is basically village oriented. Fakir Mohan began his literary work taking the characters from the village area. He was the only artist to create extraordinary literature on them, Before him no other man had taken this daring step in the literary history of Odisha. In his novels and stories he gives a clear picture of the Odia society. In the social novels of Fakir Mohan the living standard of the 19th century Odisha, its culture and mannerism have been vividly portrayed. [23]

Chhamana Athaguntha is written in the common language of the day-to-day life, picking up the general life. In this novel, the social life of the Odias was confined to villages. At that time a new zamindar class arose in the society. In it is described the tyranny, exploitation of the zamindars in the society and the mention of their luxurious life. A cruel picture of the oppression of the English and non Odias on the illiterate Odias is seen in it. The picture of bad instincts of widows and corrupt women in the society is also portrayed in the novel.

In Fakir Mohan's 'Lachhama ', the destruction of feudal civilization and monarchy in the name of anarchy have been reflected how life and property of Odisha was at stake due to the cruel oppression of the Marathas. He presented in the novel how the attitude of the people of the society of the Maratha race changed is also indicated in it.[24]

A change in this condition of the society is observed in the novel 'Mamu'. In it the attraction to town, unbecoming Love for English education, greed for service are painted. Two institutions of urban society debauchery and prostitution are explored at length. The rise of an educated middle class at the end of 19 th century and the beginning of 20 th century is narrated in the novel 'Prayaschitta' The social reformation by the educated youth in the light of English civilization and thought is reflected in it. The picture of the consequence of building a new tradition breaking the ancient one of the society is vividly drawn in this novel.

In the stories of Fakir Mohan., two types of society, ancient and modern are seen. The social picture like exploitation of the landlord robbery and hypocrisy in the name of religion are described. Disrespect and negligence of the modern educated youth to their superiors' addiction and the use of broom for its remedy are portrayed in the stories in a hilarious manner. Fakir Mohan has narrated the vocation of different castes of the society in his novels and stories. He described in his story better how Rebati was laid on casteism in 19th century. The Brahmin society and its deterioration was exhibited in the novel Chhaman Athaguntha.[25]

During his life-time he wrote a number of essays, poems stories novels and autobiography. He encouraged others to write. Here one example may be noted: Arnapurna Devi, a woman poet of Odisha showed some of her literary works at the time if her first stage to a great litterateur of Odisha. She was advised by him to stop writing and not to publish the same but Fakir Mohan had told her, "Ma, you do not hear anybody's word, you go on writing". It was Fakir Mohan's speciality. From this it is known how much Fakir Mohan had love for Odia literature. He advised everybody to keep writing in order to save mother tongue.

He had a reformative zeal which he indicated in his writings. He wanted the reformation which would suit the society. He was not in favour of speedy reformation.

Fakir Mohan's autobiography "*Atma Jiban Charita*" is not only the first of its kind in Odia but remains the best and most interesting in Indian languages. Moreover, it is as readable as any of his novels and exciting short-stories. *Vyasa Kavi's* novels are *Chhamana Athaguntha* (1902), *Lachhama* (1903), *Mamu* (1913) and *Prayaschita* (1915). *Lachhama* is a historical novel set against the backdrop of Maratha invasion of Odisha in the eighteenth century. The other three novels are portraits of contemporary society of Orissa. All these four novels depict the social history of Odisha from the eighteenth to early twentieth century.

5.1 CHHAMANA ATHAGUNTHA

The contrast between temporal and spiritual justice is the theme of Chhamana Athaguntha. Temporal justice as embodied in the local police and legal profession was venal, corrupt and inadequate. Local graft is typified by the village constable. Gobara Jena, a Pan (untouchable), living in the Dom quarters of the village. In league with Mangaraja and acknowledged thieves, Gobara Jena insured himself against arrest by taking presents to the entire police station staff, when making his monthly report. When finally implicated in a series of robberies, he got himself acquitted by bribing the Munshi. He abused his authority by intimidating the villagers into taking turns in feeding him each night. If a villager refused, Gobara took the night off and mysteriously during his absence that villager's home was robbed. Gobara was a sly, cunning, untrustworthy rascal and it was he who eventually betrayed Mangaraja.

Legal corruption is personified by the lawyer, Rama Lal. Fakir Mohan's description of Managaraja's home, one of his many digs at the legal profession, hints at the opulence of lawyers and the illegality with which that opulence was acquired.

"At first sight Mangaraja's mansion could easily be taken either for the home of a western-educated lawyer or for the spoils of four score other homes.

Rama Lal and his breed has made Justice one more commodity to be bought and sold. At the end of a long interview with Mangaraja, Rama Lal said,

"Well Mangaraja, we've got to buy them all, from the peon to the office-in-charge. It's a very tricky case. No other lawyer would touch it for less than ten thousand. It's only because I'm different that' I'm taking it on. How can I let you down, when you look on me as a guardian? Right, I'll bear the whole cost, which won't be a penny less than ten thousand.

Mortgage your estate to me. It won't cost the full value, of course. I'll give you a detailed account, when you're acquitted."

The full inadequacy of temporal justice was, however, epitomized in the British judge, whose very unscrupulousness worked in Mangaraja's favour. Though convinced that Mangaraja was a black-guard and scoundrel, who had brought tragedy on Bhagia and Saria by defrauding them of their small parcel of land, the judge nevertheless insisted that Mangraja could be tried only on the charges preferred against him and that on the relevant evidence Mangaraje was innocent of all but of them, the theft of the cow Neta.

Despite the inadequacy of temporal justice, there was however, another law (dharma), whose workings were inexorable.

Thus none could escape the consequences of their misdeeds. Campa who plotted the defrauding of Bhagia and Saria suffered the most hideous heath in the whole of Odia literature. Govinda, the barber-lover, who murdered her, was eaten alive by a crocodile. Gobara Jena, who had rigged evidence of murder to frame Mangaraja, was jailed for perjury and slaughtered by the Doms, he had helped Mangaraja to get falsely convicted of theft. And finally Mangaraja found himself on a murder charge facing a Munshi who bore him a grudge for failing to pay a promised bribe. The Munshi determined to prosecute for the maximum penalty, but as luck would have it. Mangaraja was acquitted. Thought escaping the hangman, Mangaraja did nevertheless at the hands of those same Doms he and Gobara had betrayed.

5.2 LACHHMA

'Lachhama' is a historical novel. It is created on the basis of the social and political history of 19th century Odisha. It is a story of struggle against the reactionary forces. The war between the Mughals and the Marathas from 1741 to 1751 has been described in the novel. The oppression of the Marathas, the war between Alivardi Khan, Nawab of Bengal and Bhaskar Pandit, the Maratha leader, and the murder of Bhaskar Pandit all are historical events. Bhaskar Pandit, Alivardi Khan, Murshid Qulikhan are the historical characters. The places like Raibania fort, Haldipada, Murshidabad, Phulwara etc. are the historical places. Badal Singh are historical characters which is doubtful till now.[26]

5.3 MAMU

Mamu continues the theme of justice, but concentrates on reform rather than punishment. Chhamana Athaguntha had raised the possibility of Mangaraja's repentance in a memorable passage, where Fakir Mohan, citing Christian, Brahma, Vaisnavite and other Hindu scriptures, had meditated on the make-up of man and the causes of change in his personality. Fakir Mohan sympathized with Mangaraja and his self-caused sufferings, and held with Sanatana Brahma Dhrama that sin (papa) was odious, not sinners.

The similarities between Chhamana Athaguntha and Mamu in theme, plot and characterization are great. Mamu's Natabara Das is a mere middle class version of Mangaraja, but the class difference was crucial, for Fakir Mohan believed that class and morality were interdependent. For various reason the rich and the poor exaggerated the importance of wealth to the detriment of both their own souls and society. Given a sufficiency of means as in the middle-classes and the benefits of moral instruction in childhood, men have every chance of becoming good.

Enjoying these advantages, Natabara ought to have remained incapable. Poverty had driven Mangaraja into crime, but Natabara was driven there by temperament. He was 'crafty and pleasure-loving', and even in childhood had shown 'signs of meanness' .He had become convinced that 'life's sole purpose was the acquisition of wealth' which did not come 'like the rains from heaven; but 'had to be taken from others by cunning. That scrupulousness known as Dharma was, 'he felt' 'only for the idle and the stupid.' "These convictions had made Natabara materialistic atheist to whom no crime was impossible.

It is pointed that Fakir Mohan again meditates on the inadequacy of the law. Compared to conscience, the law was a poor deterrent. A belief in an all-seeing, omniscient God, a sense of morality, and a tender and lively conscience could check a man's propensity to crime, but a fear was easily circumvented by a mere increase in caution. Thus given materialistic atheism and cunning circumspection a man might, like Natabara, be tempted to think he could commit the crime with impunity.[27]

Nevertheless, Natabara was not beyond redemption. He came 'of stainless stock' and therefore had some slight purity secreted in his heart. Released at the first touch of adversity this secretion stifled his materialistic atheism. It would seem that Fakir Mohan muses in order to return man's erring soul to the path of rectitude, God sends a powerful directive in the form of adversity.

Consequently, when remanded in custody, Natabara was moved to repentance and a renewed faith in God, which at first lent him a startling composure and dignity in accepting the consequences of his misdeeds, but which later became so intense as to precipitate madness. Thus in the event Natabara did not reform, but the basis of reform had been there, a middle-class background, sound heredity and moral instruction in childhood. In Fakir Mohan's final novel Prayaschitta it will be seen how these advantages tended ultimately to dispose a man towards repentance, reform and finally expiation.

5.4 PRAYASCHITTA

Prayascitta continues on more or less the theme Mamu, but concentrates on the conflicting claims of the world and the spirit. Govinda Chandra, the central character, is a younger, more romantic version of Natabara Dasa. He is upper-middle-class, Western educated, atheistic and crime-prone. Like Natabara Dasa, Govinda too is touched by adversity, in his case by a particularly savage beating, which lands him in hospital. There, while recuperating, he reviews his past life. His studies of Western philosophy had inclined him to atheism. Atheism had made him arrogant and scornful of good advice. There's no crime an atheist is incapable of. Only the fear of the law restrains him his friend Doctor Sukanta Ray, had once bluntly told him, but Govinda Candra had ignored the warning. Now, however, having deceived his father, precipitated his wife's suicide and his mother's grief-stricken death, he was consumed with remorse and determined to dedicate his life to meditation on God's name.

His father, Vaisnava Charana, dissuades him, however. Men, he said had a duty to both the world and the spirit. It was completely proper that, as long as they were physically able, they should try to increase their happiness and comfort in lawful and socially approved ways. This was as God intended. But later it was equally proper that they should strive to improve their souls. But for Govinda Chandra that time had not yet come. It was too early for him to abandon the world. Dharma comprised both worship and service. Mankind was God's family. To serve man was therefore to worship God. God had granted Govinda great wealth, ability and knowledge. Use it to spread education, to tend the sick, and to secure the needy on an estate: Vainava Charana urged. To become an ascetic would in his case be selfish waste of all the capabilities granted by the grace of God.

The narrative style of Fakir Mohan Senapati's fictions has outlived his time, yet before entering into writing prose fictions and other forms of prose literature, Fakir Mohan wrote poetry for about forty years. His first indigenous venture in poetry writing "Utkala Bhramana" got published in 1982. In spite of being a tale of journey, this work included praise and criticism of many contemporary personalities expressed in a very interesting and lucid manner. Apart from it, Odia literature has been enriched by his collections of many lyrical poetry like "Pushpamala", "Upahar", Pujaphula",

Dhul" "Prarthana" and "Abasara Basare". He also contributed to Odia epic through his work "Boudhabatra" He translated the two great mythological works "the Ramayana and "The Mahabharata" from original Sanskrit to Odia language. For his translation of the Mahabharata, he became known as Vyasakabi Fakir Mohan. His great erudition and unmatched talent as a writer so much impressed the king of Bamanda and he was awarded with the honour of "Saraswati" by the king's court.

So far as prose literature in Odia is concerned, Fakir Mohan made it resplendent with his short stories and fictions. His fictions "Chhamana Athaguntha, "Mamu" and "Prayaschitta" were based on contemporary social issues while his "Lachhama" was based on Marahatta history of Odisha.

Fakir Mohan Senapati has drawn on his canvas of Odia literature, very candid pictures of the contemporary Odia society raising strong voice of resent and protest against the social dogmas and blind beliefs. He never hesitated to criticize anomalies in any form in the social life. The so called elites of the English educated youths, touts and sycophants, zamindars, miserly businessmen, police personals and even the Brahmins, Karanas, Muslim weavers lacking in social ethics became victims of his vitriolic criticism. In fact, he was quite fearless in exposing corruption and social injustice in the society.

Fakir Mohan might not have written too many short stories, yet what ever he has written in this genre have been invaluable gems in the garland of his literary production. In " Odia Sahityara Itihas", Mayadhar Mansingh says, "Even though the short stories and novels written by Fakir Mohan are only a few in number, each one of them opens a new vision of our social life before us."

Litterateur Surendra Mahanty opines, "Among all the Indian languages, Fakir Mohan is the pioneer of Short story writing. Whatever stories written by other Indian authors before Fakir Mohan, did not have the artistic excellence that Fakir Mohan's stories manifest nor, were they of any superior literary values in comparision to Fakir Mohan's stories."

Prof. Brundaban Chandra Acharya in "Odia Sahityara Sankshipta Parichaya" writes, "Fakir Mohan happens to be a modern short story writer in its true sense."

The lively style of illustration of the social and educational situation in the contemporary Odia society can easily be seen through the short stories of Fakir Mohan. [28]

5.4 LACHHMANIA

In the year 1868 the story "Lachhamania" was published in the magazine "Bodhadayini" Published from Balasore, Since this magazine has gone into the abyss of being forgotten, not much information about the story is available and so it is still a matter of debate among the scholars as to whether this was the first short story fulfilling all the merits of the genre.

5.5 REBATI

The short story Rebati was written after Lachchmania. Due to unavailability of Lachhmania, Rebati has been recognized by literary scholars as Fakir Mohan's first short story. This story is surcharged with the emotions of pathos. This story demonstrats the clash between the older tradition of belief and the new. Jejema (grandmother) in the story represents the old and the orthodox belief that stand against women's education. On the other hand Basudev and Rebati represent the social and psychological change that slowly and steadily made inroads in Odisha due to the advent of modernism through western culture. Some critics opine that Fakir Mohan has advocated against women education. But such criticism is a clear travesty of truth since Fakir Mohan as a conscious individual has only tried to expose the contemporary mind set of the male dominated orthodox older generation who were completely against any form of modernization. Modernisation, they believed, was a social evil. In fact Fakir Mohan has been very categorical in his advocacy in favour of women education. Rebati the young girl child, thus, rejects her grand mother's plea against her education and says to her father that she would study. The grand mother though dogmatically attributes the death of Vasudev to Rebati's education; Fakir Mohan does not accept this. His contemporary society was replete with blind beliefs and disaster in any form was attributed to some blind belief of the other. Fakir Mohan only tries to show that Vasudev's death was only incidental upon the epidemic of cholera that broke out in the locality and was in no way related to Rebati's education. The sudden death of Vasudev comes as a severe shock to Rebati so much so that she is mentally and emotionally broken and she silently becomes aloof from the happy side of life. Consequent upon the death of Rebati, the Grandmother also dies ending the story in a very sad note. This compelling story makes the reader think deeply about the social evils that engulfed Fakir Mohan's contemporary society. Reading of Rebati easily demonstrates that Fakir Mohan though accommodates his contemporary social evils; he does so only with a view to rejecting them as he is convinced that all such social evils are the result of lack of education and social awareness.

5.6 PATENT MEDICINE

Along with being an excellent story teller, Fakir Mohan was also a social reformer in the sense that he was very severe in criticizing any thing wrong in the contemporary society. Though his narratives have humour at the superficial level, they always have a very strong under current of social criticism. Patent Medicine is a story that tells us about the role of a woman to cure the contemporary social malady of alcoholism so rampant in the society. She was various methodious and with her presence of mind she is able to reform her alcoholic and misdirected husband. A woman is an epitome of love, forgiveness, generosity and selfless service. At the same time she can also be strong and ruthless like Chandi and Durga when the situation demands. The story patent Medicine shows how women can have control over her family making it happy and beautiful with her calculated and innovative ways of her learning and education. Patent Medicine very dramatically tells s how Chandramani's wife Sulochana does not even hesitate to bash up her alcoholic husband with a broom to bring him back to the right path.

5.7 RANDI PUA ANANTA

This story again is a tragic one. Here we come across how the careless, ill directed and irresponsible son Ananta still pampered quarrelsome mother Debaki, a widow has a change of mind. Ananta relentlessly troubles the village people and also the village teacher. But the same Ananta is transferred when it comes to saving the village from flood. He tries to block the flow of flood water in to the village and in the process he sacrifices his own life. This story tells us that true values of education is not in getting higher education or certificates of recognition but it is there in the productive use of one's wisdom and generosity. Ananta may not have the degrees of formal education but finally his mental transformation present him as having the true value of education.

5.8 GARUDI MANTRA

This is a family story written in a very lighter vein. It is a story of a zamidar's family which does not allow the newly wed zamidar's son to meet his wife during day time. So the zamidar's son makes a plan. He frightens his wife with an artificial snake and then he himself tries to cure his wife by chanting of "mantras in the guise of witch doctor.

5.9 ADHARMA BITTA

This story is about a corrupt businessman who is also a money lender. He amasses a lot of money and property through corrupt and evil means. Finally he is drowned in the abated Mahanadi with all his fortunes. Yet due to the honesty and pious nature and activities of his wife and son, the son and the daughter-in-law are saved from being drowned to death. The often quoted Odia proverb "Adharma bitta bahed badhuta-Jiba bele jaye mula sahita" (Property earned through corrupt means increases manifold but when it is lost every pie is lost) has been justified in this story. The story letter indicates here that the surest way to indentify between a corrupt and an honest person is through proper education. Education is the invincible weapon though which it becomes easy to identify and understand blind beliefs, conspiracies and exploitation in the right way. This story evince the fact that property earned through evil means is temporary and that through education we can face the challenges of any problems and find ways to riggle out of it.

5.10 BIREI BISHALA

This story is written in the back drop of purely rural setting and rural system of behaviour and activity. Piteipatra Apatya is the maternal uncle of the village lad Birei an orphan. One can easily compare the uncle with the mythological character Kamsa. Birei stays with his uncle after he loses his parents. The uncle has a covetous eye on the property of Birei. He is not treated well in his uncle's house. They do not show any love and affection to him. Birei finally decides to leave his uncle's home and go back to his own village to take care of his property. After he leaves his uncle's home, his irresponsible cousin the uncle's son squanders the family property. This way the cousin even steals cows and goes to jail. As a result, the uncle and the aunt become beggars and then take shelter with Birie to spend the rest of life. Birie also shows great character and generosity to forgive them and take care of them

5.11 SABHYA ZAMINDAR

Fakir Mohan was aware of both positive and the negative side of the influence of the British Culture. So he has never hesitated to welcome and accommodate the positive influence and very critically dispel the negative influence. He has been of the opinion that whereas it is acceptable to accommodate the brighter side of the British culture, any blind and thoughtless imitation of it should be discouraged. Sabhya Zamindar tells us the story of how the blind imitation of British culture has ruined the family Zamindar Gopal Chandra Mahapatra is an ideal character. But his son Rajib comes into the company of some bad people and loses his own character and integrity. In the name of being modern he becomes alcoholic and gets involved is acts of debauchery. In the process he loses his property and becomes an employee to support himself. Fakir Mohan here indicates that it is highly dangerous to lose one's wisdom due to wealth and property because the misuse of them leads one to invite days of suffering.

5.12 DAK MUNSHI

Dak Munshi very candidly demonstrates how the English educated so called civilized young man Gopal ignores and ill-treats his father Hari Singh. Since Hari Singh is an uneducated man. It was probably not uncommon for many such English educated so called civilized youths in Fakir Mohan's contemporary Odisha to feel ashamed of giving real identity of their uneducated rustic father to their English educated friends. To give the actual identity of the father was considered loss of prestige by such people and so they did not even hesitate to call the father as the servant of the family.

In the present story Hari Singh an uneducated man from a village spends all his belongings to educate his son. As a result he becomes a pauper and his English educated son becomes a post master. Having nothing to depend upon in his old age he has to depend on his son and stay with him. But this helpless old man is unwanted in the family of his son for whose education and better life he sacrificed every thing. This moving situation recreated by Fakir Mohan of his own time inspired the reader a great deal. Education disciplines and polishes the life and behaviour of an individual. But in Dak Munshi we come across a contradiction. A false imitation of the western culture and the Sahib culture have made Gopal, completely and almost disdainfully reject his own roots to adopt to the false glory of the alien culture. This has made him a person sans sympathy, sans being humane and sans being responsive to responsibility. Through this story, Fakir Mohan has tried to enlighten the contemporary youths not to dispel and disregard their roots which are full of love and respect for our parents and fellow brothers and sisters. Education, English or otherwise never teaches us to dehumanize ourselves. It is only our false nature that does it.

5.13 SUNA BOHU

It is purely a family story of a middle class family. It tells us the story of a newly married daughter-in-law who being an educated lady considers herself as the mistress and hates to do any house hold work. Her arrogance is changed under the influence of the wise married daughter of the family and the daughter-in-law eventually becomes a "Suna Bohu" (A good Daughter-in-law).

5.14 DHULIA BABA

This story deals with the practices and activities of a fraud self claimed saint. The writer hints at the fact that this story is partially based on truth. How these self- claimed fraud saints take advantage of the innocent god-fearing people and exploit them enormously to amass wealth and yet how such saint end up with extreme punishment is the theme of this story.

5.15 PATHOI BOHU

This story is based on the situations resulting out of lack of education in a rural family. The hesitancy among rural women to get educated leads them to suffer a great deal after marriage. In this story the uneducated wife is not able to respond and reciprocate to what her educated husband says or needs. This leads to severe dislocation of family peace. Fakir Mohan tries to say here through this story that women need to be educated for peace and prosperity of a family and the society. A progressive family and a nation greatly depend on women's education.

5.16 MADHA MAHANTYNKA KANYASUNA

Often certain socially accepted maxims come true. In this story an old man gives in marriage to his young daughter with an old man. After that he falls seriously ill and succumbs to death. This story demonstrates the social situation where due to greed and to keep their property safe some people give in marriage to their daughters with ineligible persons. They consider the girl child to be a curse on them and gleefully get rid of their girl childhood. The social evil that a girl child is a burden t the family and that she should be given in marriage by any means is highlighted in the story and the story teller severely criticizes it.

5.17 BAGALA BAGULI

A human emotion of love and mutual understanding is not confined to any class, caste, race or religion. Fakir Mohan in this story unequivocally shows this truth trough the two characters Bagala and Bagali. The husband and wife Sapna and Chemi are uneducated and they belong to a lower caste. In spite of it they are religious and are well conversant on the religious books. The husband and wife love each other so deeply that love itself becomes sublime in their relationship. They live together and die together. Their relationship is an example for the new generation.

Apart from all these short stories Fakir Mohan has also written a few more stories full of satire like “Ashcharya Swapna”, “Muhare Nia, “Bohu Roga”. In these stories particularly is Ascharya Swapna and Muhare Nia, Fakir Mohan unambiguously satirizes the alcoholism, prostitution and all kinds of amoral activities so rampant among the so called English educated youths during his time.

Fakir Mohan also wrote in the pen name- nom de plume .... Of Dhurjati and at times ‘Shree’. His story ‘Kula Kuntala’ was written in his pen name Dhurjati and was published in the Utkala Sahitya. ‘Kabitwa Bisarjana’, ‘Suna Nakachana’, ‘Punarmushikabhaba’, ‘Mouna Mouni’ were the stories written in his pen name Shree.

Fakir Mohan through his stories shows that noble acts are always benevolently efficacious while evil acts are always malevolent in result. He clearly says through many of his stories that it is only through proper education that a healthy society can be built. The powerful writings of Fakir Mohan not only created a strong base Odia literature, it also opened new horizons for Odia literature to strive forward.

Apart from poetry, short stories, and novels Fakir Mohan has also written quite a few essays, travel stories, suspense stories and humorous stories and essays. His essays normally contain the values of education. Among his suspense and humorous stories are "Suspense" "Station Masteranka apuraba Go Bhakti", "Bahara Bhati", Jani Krutabidya, Lekhaka" Hitopadesha Rahasya, "Khos Galpa", "Puja Rahasya", "Bad Dina", "Bai Nacha", "Naba barsha rahasya",Shri Sri Abadhan (Abishkara) "Stabaka, Paramartha, Tatwabichar" Ruturaj Basanta "Smarta and Vaishnaba" "Veer Bangali, Ganesha Chaturthi, Shri Shri Durgapuja, Municipaliti, Kedara Nagar, Manaba Tatwa, Kalpna O Jalpna, Bai Mahanti Panji, Ranga Rasa and Nananka Panji.

Fakir Mohan has also written some important literary testimonials and essays which deal with the various social problems and needs of the society. Among them are:

'Mandira Munankara Kusticita Murti', 'Gada Jatara Raja Mane', 'Odishara Adhunika Abastha', 'Aya Dekhi Kara Byaye Pachhaku Kale Tana Tune Hue', 'Bramhanda', 'Ambhamanankara Kabiraj', 'Baha Bibada', 'Pruthak Na Hua', 'Nukhila Munda Kahun Telia Heba', 'Krushi Banijya Dwara Deshara', 'Unnti Hue Chakiri Dwara Nuhe', 'Dhumketu', 'Nimna Shiksya Samparkiya Gotie Paramarsha', 'Prakruta Ekata Kahaku Kuhanti', 'Odishara Bartamana abastha', 'Dhenkanalara Ki Durdasha', 'Odishara Dahi chudakhiya Brahmane', 'Shakya Sighnka Stree Gopa', 'Jati Samskara Andolana', 'Swabhaba O Danda', 'Milana', 'Ingraji Shikhya', 'Ashcharya Upachikitsa' 'Hindu mananka Upanibesha', 'Jahara Bala Tahara Fala', 'Pralobhanati Koushala', 'Kabuli Hindu', 'Deshiya Sahityonnati', 'Yoga Shastra', 'Utkala bhasha ra Bhuta Bhabishyata', 'Jamayet Babajinka

Utpatti', 'Ali Malika', 'Shri Kshetrare Chaitanya Mahaprabhu', 'Kabi Gopal Krushna Pattnaik','Kabi Michau', 'Madhusudan Datta ebang Meghnad Badha Kabya', 'Tridharma Samanwaya', 'Tukram', 'Gotra', 'Arata', 'Shudra O Vedadhikara', 'Ghodara Kurukuri Roga', 'Bangali lani' and 'Meghnad Badha Samalochanara Samalochana' etc. [29]

Fakir Mohan's literature has stood out as invaluable boon to the growth and development of Odia literature. His Philosophic base as a man of literature was strongly rooted in his passionate vision as a social reformer which could be manifested in terms of reality only through the spread of proper education and perusing our just and appropriate culture.

REFERENCES

1. Prasbhu Kalyan Mohapatra, Orissa Review, April,2005 P.22
2. Ibid.P.23
3. Ibid. P.24
4. Fakir Mohan Senapati, (2006): *Six Acres and a Third*, translated, Rabi Shankar Mishra, Satya P Mohanty, Jatindra K Nayak, Paul St-Pierre, Penguin Books, New Delhi, PP.23-26.
5. Satya Prasad Mohanty, (2006): 'Introduction' in *Six Acres and a Third,* Penguin, New Delhi, pp 1-31.
6. Natabar Samantaray,Vyasakadi fakir mohan (oriya) 1972. Bhubaneswar. P.70.
7. Surendra Mohanty, Fakir Mohan samikshya (oriya) .1972 .cuttack. p.234.
8. Ibid,p.227.
9. Ibid,p.64.
10. B.K.Satpathy (ed),op.cit.p.28.
11. Surendra Monanty ,Fakir Mohan samikshya(oriya),1972.Cuttack. PP.62-63.
12. Ibid,p.233.
13. Braja Mohan Mahanty. Oriya sahityara adhunika jaga, part (oriya)1966. Cuttack.pp.90-91.
14. Ibid,p.106.
15. Srinibas Mishra. Adhunika oriya Gadhya sahity (oriya), 1978. Cuttack, p.145
16. Braja Mohan Mohanty,Oriya sahityara adhunika juga,Par l(oriya), 1966, Cuttack,p.105.

17. N.Mohanty, Oriya Nationalism, Quest for a united Orissa, 1982, New Delhi. P.73

18. Nayar Kuldip (1975): *India after Nehru*, Vikas Publishing House, Delhi.
PP-27-29

19. Bipinchandra Pal, (1945): *The Brahmo Samaj and the Battle for Swaraj in India,* Sadharan Brahmo Samaj, Calcutta.P.56

20. Biswamoy Pati, (2001): *Situating Social History: Orissa (1800-1997),* Orient Longman, New Delhi.P.97

21. Rabi Shankar Mishra and Jatindra Kumar Nayak (1991): 'Literature and Society' in *Economic and Political Weekly,* 26(3), p 136.

22. Mukherjee, Meenakshi (1985): *Realism and Reality: The Novel and Society in India,* Oxford University Press, New Delhi.PP.12-14

23. Fakir Mohan Senapati, Autobiography,(Oriya),1981, Cuttack P-4

24. B.K. Satpathy (ed), Fakir Mohan His Life and literature, 1984, Balasore,P.2

25. Fakir Mohan Senapati .op.cit p.6

26. Golak Chandra Mohapatra, Senapati Fakir Mohan (Oriya), 1986, Balasore .p.5

27. B.K.Satpathy (ed.), op.cit pp.36-37

28. Fakir Mohan Senapati , op.cit .pp.5.6

29. Natabar Samantaray, Oriya Sahitvara Itihas, (Oriya) 1964, Bhubaneswar p. 375.

◆◆◆

CHAPTER-VI

FAKIR MOHAN'S PHILOSOPHY OF LIFE

CHAPTER VI

FAKIR MOHAN'S PHILOSOPHY OF LIFE

Novelists are also philosophers. Odia novelist Fakir Mohan Senapati is no exception, and yet he cannot be treated as a philosopher in the accepted sense of the term since he has not left behind him any systematic statement of his thought. However, his literary creations, experiences of life, and correspondence with his contemporaries reveal his philosophy. Fakir Mohan's philosophy is deep-rooted in Indian idealism and spiritualism. The important facets of Fakir Mohan's philosophy are presented in the following paragraphs. [1]

"When there is the bustle of progress everywhere, will Utkal be still in slumber?" This line from Fakirmohan's first original poem *Utkal Bhraman* (Tours of Orissa) not only epitomises his literary overview but also depicts his flare for Odia nationalism. Fakir Mohan Senapati, regarded as the father of modern Odia literature, dedicated his entire life for the progress of Odia language. He also played a leading role in establishing the distinct identity of Odia language and literature. So the story of Fakir Mohan is indeed the story of the "renaissance" in Odia literature. [2]

6.1 A BELIEVER IN GOD

Fakir Mohan Senapati was intellectually restless and adventurous, and had the spirit of a reformer more than that of a writer in search of literary fame. He grew up in a part of colonial India that barely registered in the consciousness of the Viceroys and their officials. But it is from this particular vantage point that he created a unique synthesis of the traditional and the contemporary, a synthesis whose power and example are relevant even today. Senapati`s critique was never merely negative; it was based on a vision of human equality and cultural diversity, of a radical humanism that was fed by a variety of religious traditions. [3]

Quite a few Odia novelists emerged in the nineteen-twenties and wrote through nineteen thirties. Chintamani Mohanty's Jugala Matha, published in 1920, speaks of the moral depravity of a spiritual person, the head of a matha, whose indulgence in wine and women leads to his expulsion from the math. He eventually settles down at Puri and expiates his sins.Mohanty's Tanka Gacha, published in 1923, deals with the problem of migrant labour, the predicament of the poor Odia's who run away to the tea gardens of Assam in search of work and livelihood. Bula Fakira, published in 1924, is the story of a prodigal youth who runs away to Calcutta and through trials and tribulations reforms himself and leads a happy life. This novel also depicts the state of misery and humiliation of young widows in traditional Oriya families. A common trait in all the novels of Chintamani Mohanty is his deep concern for the rural poor. His novels clearly reflect his missionary zeal for social reform and rural development. The two novelists who may be treated as the most worthy successors of Fakir Mohan are Upendra Kishore Das whose novel Malajanha, published in 1922, is indisputably a modern\ classic, and Baishnab Charan Das whose novel Manemane, published in 1927, deals with an\ unconventional theme of love between a married woman and a young man. The plot of Malajanha centres round a young girl Sati who is forced into marriage with an ugly old man living with a concubine. The marriage eventually ends in tragic separation and Sati finds shelter with Nathanana, her childhood friend. The relationship between Sati and Nathanana is one of strong emotional bond though neither has ever spoken out to the other about the intensity of love. Sati, unable to bear the scandal concerning her and Nathanana, finally commits suicide by jumping into the river. This poignant love story is narrated in the context of life in rural Odisha infested by superstitions, narrow caste prejudices and acute poverty. Women were like slaves with no mind and choice of their own and child marriages were widely prevalent. [4]

Fakir Mohan's sense of humour and irony has remained unsurpassed in Odia literature and it is his characteristic style which made him popular with a wide range of readers. He believed that Faith, Asceticism, Love and Devotion were four pillars that formed the base of '*Dharma*'. His faith was derived from Islam, asceticism from Buddhism, love from Christianity and devotion from Vaishnavism.[5] The formation of modern Odisha in 1936 as a linguistic province is certainly a landmark in the history of the evolution of language based states of the Indian Union. Formation of linguistic states which was accepted as a norm for re-organisation of the states of the Independent India idea had its genesis in the movement of the Odia language which broke out in around the second half of nineteenth century. As such the Odia language movement had an indelible imprint on the socio-political and cultural history of Odisha in which Fakir Mohan played a pivotal role. Due to his relentless efforts the first printing press of Balasore was established in the year 1868. [6]

Fakir Mohan's three novels Chhamana Athaguntha, Mamu and Prayaschitta reveal the gradual evolution and growth of his consciousness. In Chhamana Athaguntha, Managaraja is an evil man from the lower classes. He is thoroughly vicious and is punished both through the courts and through his victims by a kind of natural or poetic justice.[7] In Mamu Natabar does repent and is also on the verge of reform, but goes insane under the stress of conscience. Nevertheless, reform was possible in Natabara, for he was from middle-class and had enjoyed the advantage of religious instruction in childhood. In Prayaschitta everyone eventually repents and reforms. Sadanand alone goes to prison. The rest punish themselves through their consciences and strive to atone for their misdeeds by dedicating the remainder of their lives to Dharma through the service of either God or man, both of which constitute worship. Thus Chhamana Athaguntha, Mamu and Prayascitta constitute a trilogy on temporal and spiritual Justice, in the course of which Fakir Mohana gradually moves away from temporal law in favour of eternal law (Dharma), and the term crime becomes imperceptibly replaced by the term 'sin'. [8]

Fakir Mohana therefore wanted a return to the old system. Knowing this to be politically impossible, he could achieve it only in fiction. So the authentic realism of early works like Chhamana Athaguntha and Rebati was usurped by visions of his ideal society in later works like Prayascitta and Bagula Baguli. Chhamana Athaguntha and Rebati had reeked of materialism, in which virtue choked and died, but in Bagula Baguli the whole of society was bathed in generosity and good principles, emanating from the nightly readings of the Puranas in the village Bhagavata Ghara. [9]

In some other short stories like Garudi Mantra and Pathoi Bohu Fakir Mohan also pleads for the desirability of education for women and their emancipation. Similarly, the hypocrisy and different kinds of oppression and deception prevalent in the traditional Hindu society have formed the subject matter of many of his short stories. In Birei Bisala and Madhu Mahantinka Kanyasuna he comes down heavily upon the hypocrisy as well as upon the inhuman and ignoble practice of bird-selling prevalent among the people belonging to certain castes of society. In Dhulia Baba he has exposed a religious fraud. On the whole, in the works of Fakir Mohan and especially in his short stories, a dismal and decadent picture of the traditional Hindu society has been presented on which he has passed a severe stricture. [10]

Fakir Mohan Senapati had strong faith in God. He himself has confirmed it in his brief autobiography. His long narratives Mauna Mouni, Dhuliababa, underline the greatness of human life and emphasise the sacred influence of God on the life of man. The important characters of Fakir Mohan Senapati's literature are endowed with sincere devotion to God. [11]

Fakir Mohan Senapati believed in God as the ultimate reality and surrendered himself to God. He regarded God as the universal soul. According to Fakir Mohan Senapati, God is the creator. He is the cause of everything. Fakir Mohan Senapati considered God as the arbitrator of our fate. To him, God is omnipotent, omnipresent and omniscient. Like Swami Dayananda Saraswati, Fakir Mohan Senapati also regarded God as the creator, maintainer and destroyer of the cosmos. Fakir Mohan Senapati not only believed in God but also stressed on the realization of God. According to him bhakti (devotion) is the only and ultimate way of realization of God.[12]

6.2 A STAUNCH IDEALIST

Fakir Mohan Senapati was a staunch idealist. Idealism formed the base of his life and literature. Like any other platonic idealist Fakir Mohan Senapati also believed in God (discussed in section 6.1). Fakir Mohan had deep faith in the Hindu Philosophy of life which is based on the foundation of idealism. As an idealist, he believed in certain ideals and principles, and lived to uphold and glorify those ideas throughout his life. He himself led a life based on simple living and high thinking, and never aspired for material prosperity at the cost of sacrificing his ideas of life.

Fakir Mohan Senapati was highly acclaimed in the length and breadth of Odisha for his emphasis on idealism in his literature. He never entertained the negative aspects of life, like nudity and moral indiscipline, in his literature.[13]

Fakir Mohan Senapati as an idealist, also emphasies on the significance of culture and tradition in human life. His novel and poetry sing the glory of rich Indian culture. Fakir Mohan in his essay Garudimantra, Pathoi Babu,Sana Bahu, Pathoi Bahu, observes that education should make a person familiar with the tradition and customs of his country. [14]

Fakir Mohan Senapati, through his literary creations, attempted to act as the teacher and path-shower of human society. He respected the idealistic Indian tradition by accepting morality as the didactic value of art and literature. The moral teachings contained in his works are meaningful and educative. Radhanath Rai, another great Odia poet and educationist, complimented Fakir Mohan as an honest man with a sacred character. Fakir Mohan was endowed with all moral virtues like honesty, truthfulness, comity, kindness and forgiveness. He was so honest that 'even while serving as a low-paid Amin he had the courage to testify against his employer in the court of law'. [15]

Time, taste and distance divide Odia society into a small, modern, urbanized community in touch with the world trends of a large, scattered, rural community, whose literary and cultural tastes remain largely medieval. Fakir Mohana Senapati, the founder of the modern age in Odia literature, managed miraculously to achieve popularity with both these communities the old and the new largely because his mind was steeped in the age-old culture of his race, and because in consequence his literature still had that meaningful backdrop of religion, that was the source of the perennial popularity of medieval literature with the masses. He saw the modern age in the perspective of Odisha's religious experience and his sympathies lay largely with the past. [16]

The temporal Justice is gradually rejected in the three novels Chhamana Athaguntha, Mamu and Prayascitta of Fakir Mohan. These three novels are introduced by the British. At one level, Chhamana Athaguntha is a subtle satire on British Justice. Much of the satire lies in the style. Whole chapters are delivered as if Fakir Mohan, the loquacious and discursive narrator-advocate, laboring to defend the integrity of Mangaraja. [17] Fakir Mohan's arguments, here put forward in mock-legal language and form, have an air of irrefutable logic, immense erudition and profound earnestness. Hindu and Biblical scripture, maxims of logicians and grammarians, scientific theory and jurisprudence are all ransacked for plausible bits and pieces of profundity to bolster Fakir Mohan's ramshackle arguments, but ironically the more earnestly he urges his client's cause, the more his client's hypocrisy and malpractice are laid bare. In painting Mangaraja's religious sincerity Fakir Mohan unwittingly unveils a humbug and in analyzing the causes of the cleanliness of the weaver's quarters he equally 'unwittingly' intimates that Mangaraja had stolen every single cow that quarters had possessed.[18]

The subversive function is also achieved in Chha Mana Atha Guntha by the narrator's vigorous mobilization of the resources of the many layered folk tradition of the Odia village. The novel is among other things, an enactment of the process of decay of the communal rural oral tradition of Odia society in the wake of a culture of written record and crude print. [19] A highly potent and expressive image, namely that of being pent-locked has been used in the novel to convey the sense of being entrapped in the bureaucratic culture of writing. The invocation of a many-layered idiomatic life, nourished by songs, jokes, hearsay and legends, in this context, is deeply significant.

Fakir Mohan not only exhibits a sharp sense of observation of minute details relating to the social reality of rural Odisha but also makes incisive comments on the corrupting forces that threatened the erosion of moral values in society.While Chha Mana Atha Guntha depicts the suffering and agony of the common man caused by the tyranny of the zamindars, Mamu deals with the new class of exploiters in urban Odisha whose greed for wealth leads them to ruthless villainy and cruel action. This novel is a sharp indictment of the educated youth who grew up in the colonial ambience of power and wealth and ignored all traditional moral values in the selfish interest of grabbing wealth in Prayaschitta. [20]

The social realism of the early Odia novelist Fakir Mohan Senapati is marked, among other things, by the debate over the English language and its selective appropriation by the emerging bourgeoisie in the colonial state. The response to the English language and western education in Fakir Mohan is often seen as complex and problematic. There is of course a clear disavowal of neat polarizations such as Tradition-Modernity, Orality-Literacy, and the English language-the vernacular. While education is strongly upheld as a major objective, westernization, primarily seen as propelled through the English language is often equated with the 'colonising' agenda of the colonial state. [21]

Fakir Mohan is considered as the greatest prose writer in Odia literature. But it is amazing to note that he hardly wrote any prose until he retired from administrative service.

He translated Ramayan, Mahabharat and some of the Upanishads from the original Sanskrit for which he is popularly known as *Vyasa Kavi.* He wrote poetry too, but the themes of his poems were not considered conventionally fit material for poetry. He used colloquial, spoken and rugged language of the common man which no other poet in Odia had done for centuries. Fakir Mohan wrote four novels, two volumes of short-stories and one autobiography. Besides that, he mastered the art of writing short stories for which he is also termed as *Katha Samrat* (Emperor of Shortstories) in Odia literature. Fakir Mohan's autobiography "*Atma Jiban Charita*" is not only the first of its kind in Odia but remains the best and most interesting in India languages. Moreover, it is as readable as any of his novels and exciting short-stories. [22] *Vyasa Kavi's* novels are *Chhamana Atha guntha* (1902), *Lachhama* (1903), *Mamu* (1913) and *Prayaschita* (1915). *Lachhama* is a historical novel set against the backdrop of Maratha invasion of Odisha in the eighteenth century. The other three novels are portraits of contemporary society of Odisha. All these four novels depict the social history of Odisha from the eighteenth to early twentieth century. [23]

The literary creations of Fakir Mohan Senapati directly raise the voice of morality. His short stories like Rebati, Patent Medicine, Raandipua Anantaa, Gaarudi Mantra, Adharma Bitta, Sabhya Jamidar, Ajaa Naati Kathaa, Baleswari Rahajani, Pathoi Bahu, Baleswari Panga Luna, Maadha Mohantynka Kanyaa Sunaa were written, perhaps to give a moral direction to the then society. [24] The stories are still relevant for the present day society. He has tried to prove that virtue assumes more significance than wealth in one's life. Divine wealth is spent for well being of the society and wise men worship its possessor. But demonic wealth harms people and the world is thus afraid of it.Fakir Mohan as an idealist, also believed in the three absolute values of life. Truth, Goodness and beauty. These values find reflection in all his literary work. [25]

6.3 A LOVER OF NATURE

Like the famous Indian poet Kalidasa, Odia poet Radhanath Ray and English poet William Wordsworth, Fakir Mohan Senapati was also a true lover of nature. Fakir Mohan completely discarded the traditional theme of romantic love between prince-princesses and wrote about common people and their problems in his novels. In contrast to the Sanskritised style of his contemporaries, he also used colloquial idiomatic Odia in his writings with great skill and competence. If the works of earlier novelists seemed like prose renderings of medieval kavyas, Fakir Mohan`s novels were realistic to the core. He can be favorably compared with 20th century novelists like Premchand and Bibhuti Bhusan Banerjee. [26]

The four novels of Fakir Mohan Senapati, written between 1897 and 1915, reflect the social and political conditions of Odisha during the eighteenth and nineteenth centuries. Lachama, published in 1901, is a historical romance dealing with the anarchical condition of Odisha in the wake of Maratha invasions during the eighteenth century. [27] Lachama follows the tradition of the first two Odia novels, Padmamali and Bibasini whose plots were drawn from history. Most of the characters in Lachama are non- Odia and its narrative is governed by action relating to war and military diplomacy. Narrated in the epic manner of historical romance, its declamatory style, exotic atmosphere and heroic mode set it apart from the colloquial style, local atmosphere and mock-heroic mode of the other three novels of Fakir Mohan. The urge to write this historical romance might have sprung from Fakir Mohan's preoccupation with history which had earlier led him to write two volumes of school textbooks on Indian history. [28]

In Fakir Mohan Senapati's world of letters, Nature has been personified. Fakir Mohan has treated Nature as a living character like all other human characters of his literature such as Pathoi bohu, Rebati, Suna bohu, Bagala baguli, Adharmabitta, Birai Bisal, etc. Nature thus, plays different human roles in different situations. [29]

In Fakir Mohan Senapati's subtle vision, Nature is sensitive, and possesses human virtues. It is always sympathetic to human cause, and appears to be fighting against injustice. To Fakir Mohan Senapati, nature is a tested responsive friend and a solace giver, which equally shares human emotions like sorrows and happiness. [30]

Fakir Mohan Senapati's treatment of Nature emphasizes more on the internal nature of man than the external physical objects. His uniqueness lies in the expression on the inner soul of Nature, and to make it meaningful too.

6.4 A HUMANIST

Fakir Mohan Senapati was a great lover of man as well Fakir Mohan's love for man has got reflected in his literature. He loved man and hence through his innumerable creations wanted to educate and enlighten the common people. His aim was to bring about a social revolution using literature as the instrument. As a humanist, the novelist has not wished to confine him in a narrow social order. His Dakmunsi, Patient medicine, Sabhya zamidar, Birai Bisal, Adharmabitta reveals Fakir Mohan's faith in the fatherhood of god and fatherhood of man. Fakir Mohan Senapati's love for man was so intense that in his literature, Nature has also shown sympathy to man at the time of crisis. Nature has been sensitive to human suffering. [31]

Fakir Mohan Senapati voiced his resentment against exploitation of innocent, illiterate and rural masses.

Fakir Mohan Senapati's literature clearly reveals his desire for any exploitation-free human habitation. It focuses mainly in human life and its problems. Through his literary creation the writter has made a whole-hearted attempt to create an ideal human society free from all vices, and full of all virtues. Fakir Mohan Senapati's literature is nothing but an honest effort to make people conscious by properly educating them. Fakir Mohan Senapati believed in only one religion i.e. human religion. [32]

6.5 A NATIONALIST

Natinalism is not one's love of his/her country of birth. It also implies love and regard for history, religion, language and tradition of the nation.

iterature influences national life and vice-versa. Vyasakavi Fakir Mohan Senapati also composed poetry to inculcate in people the nationalist spirit. He not only yearned for the freedom of his motherland from foreign bondage, but also worked to uphold the unity and integrity of the nation and offered his best cooperation in its advancement. To make his country free, Fakir Mohan Senapati emphasized the need for economic development, social reforms, Integration and removal of all sorts of social discrimination and political and bureaucratic exploitation. [33] His desire for social change is clearly evinced in his literature. He imagined a society free from cut-throat competition. He dreamt of a healthy social order based on cooperation, sympathy, fellow feeling, fraternity, egalitarianism, democracy, harmony and above all secularism. Fakir Mohan Senapati had realized the need and significance of a secular world order almost a century ago. Fakir Mohan Senapati considered both motherland and mother tongue as equal to mother and appealed the Indian masses to come to the rescue to their nation and language. He appealed to the people for a wholehearted devotion to Odia language. [34]

Through his writings, Fakir Mohan Senapati evinced interest on patriotism, love for language, culture and tradition. His long narratives Chhamana Atha guntha, Lachhama, Mamu and Prayaschitta and short stories like Bagala Baguli, Adharma Bitta, Birai Bisal, Purna Mushika Bhava and other creations project him as a great nationalist. [35]

Fakir Mohan's first novel, Chha Mana Atha Guntha written during 1897-1899 and published in book form in 1902, is considered as a revolutionary creation in Odia language for two important reasons. Firstly, with the emergence of this novel, the language of fiction changed from that of the pundits to that of the common man. His deft handling of the spoken language of the Odia rustics redeemed Odia prose style from the burden of Sanskrit and Bengali influences and provided a distinct literary identity to the native Odia language and vocabulary. Secondly, this novel, as well as his two novels Mamu published in 1913 and Prayaschita published in 1915, were a pioneering attempt at producing fiction of social realism in Odia language. Set in the colonial Odishan society during the early decades of the nineteenth century, Chha Mana Atha Guntha is the story of an evil landlord, Ramachandra Mangaraj, who exploits poor peasants and appropriates their property. Exploitation of the poor villagers by the zamindars and the rise of a new class of exploiters among petty officials and clerks under the British government were the two dominant traits of the Odia society during nineteenth century and early decades of the twentieth century in the three novels of social realism. [36]

"When there is the bustle of progress everywhere, will Utkal be still in slumber?" This line from Fakir Mohan's first original poem *Utkal Bhraman* (Tours of Odisha) not only epitomises his literary overview but also depicts his flare for Odia nationalism. Fakir Mohan Senapati, regarded as the father of modern Odia literature, dedicated his entire life for the progress of Odia language. He also played a leading role in establishing the distinct identity of Odia language and literature. So the story of Fakir Mohan is indeed the story of the "renaissance" in Odia literature. The name Fakir Mohan itself implies the fusion of both Muslim and Hindu communities.

Fakir Mohan Senapati's revolutionary writings maintain the high status of mother tongue intact and preserve the dignity of Odia language. In his opinion a person who has no love for his language and nation can never be an intellectual.

Fakir Mohan Senapati was not only a great lover of Odia language and Odisha, but also a great lover of India as a whole. Two important factors were responsible to influence Fakir Mohan to be a nationalist: First, the background of the place where he was born and lived and second, the back drop of the time he was living.[37]

Fakir Mohan Senapati was a liberal nationalist. Though he did not take active part in the freedom movement of India, his contribution to the movement cannot be ruled out. His revolutionary and appealing writing generated great interest among the Odia people to work in unity for the development of their mother land, mother tongue. [38]

Fakir Mohan Senapati's philosophy of life combines the essentials of many philosophical doctrines such as idealism, naturalism, humanism and nationalism. Of course, idealism is the base of his philosophy and others are mere contributory to it. As an idealist, Fakir Mohan Senapati had implicit faith in God as well as in the absolute values like truth, goodness and beauty. [39] As a lover of Nature he not only gave a prominent place to nature in his literature, but also projected it as living spirit. [40] Again as a humanist, Fakir Mohan Senapati was an ardent lover of man, and worked throughout his life for the peace and progress of human society. He strived for an exploitation free human habitation based on universal brotherhood. As a nationalist Fakir Mohan participated in the meetings of Utkal Union conference and played an active role in the movement to establish Odia as an dependent language, and Odisha as a separate province. Truly speaking, Fakir Mohan's philosophy of life is eclectic in nature. [41]

REFERENCES

1. P.Bhattacharya, Maa Evevi Acchanti (translated into Oriya by Jayanti Rai) Jaipur. Matrusadan, 1980. PP. 28-34
2. P.Patnaik, Gangadhar Sahitya Parikrama, Cuttack : Diamond Publishers, 1985, PP. 203-216
3. N.R.S. Saxena, Principles of Education, Meerunt: International Publishing House, 1987, P. 308
4. S.P. Chaube, Recent Educational Philosophers in India, Agra: Ram Prasad & Sons publishers, 1967, P/ 52
5. Ibid., P. 16
6. P.Patnaik, op, cit., PP. 207-208
7. Swami Vivekananda, "The ideal of Karma Yoga", Selections from the Complete Works of Swami Vivekananda, Calcutta: Advaita Ashram, 1994, PP. 28-37
8. P. Patnaik, op. cit., P. 205
9. B.C.Naik, Makers of Indian Literature : Fakir Mohan Senapati ,New Delhi; Sahitya Academy, 1996,PP.54-96
10. Jitendra Naryan Pattnaik, Rise of the Oriya Novel:1897-1930, Orissa Review, Vol. L III, No. I, Bhubaneswar, Nov.2007, PP. 46-48
11. Ibid., P .50
12. Dr. Narayan Panda, Fakir Mohan Senapatii:The Harbinger of Renaissance in Odia literature: Orissa Review, Vol. III, No. I, Bhubaneswar, January-2012, PP. 24-25.
13. Ibid., P .27.

14. Jitendra Naryan Pattnaik,Life and time of Fakir Mohan Senapati, Orissa Review, Vol. II, No. I, Bhubaneswar, February-March-2008, PP. 56-59

15. Ibid., P .60.

16. Krushan Ch.Behera,, and Debendra K. Dash, Eds. *Fakirmohan Granthabali (Vol-I).*Cuttack: Grantha Mandira, 2000.

17. John Boulton, V. *Phakirmohan Senapati: His Life and Prose Fiction.* Bhubaneswar:Orissa Sahitya Akademi, 1993.

18. Tapas K. Chakrabarti, "Fakirmohananka Upanyasar Bhitibhumi" in *Sahitya.* Ed.Kosala Sahitya Samaj. Cuttack: Friends' Publishers, 1972.

19. Sudhir Chandra, *The Oppressive Present: Literature and Social Consciousness in Colonial India.* New Delhi: OUP, 1992.

20. Partha Chatterjee, *Nationalist Thought and the Colonial World: A Derivative Discourse?* New Delhi: OUP, 1986.

21. P. Patnaik, op.cit., PP. 171 – 183.

22. B.C.Naik, op. cit., P. 38.

23. U.S.Singh, "Meher Sahityare Samjika Angikar Vaddhata", The Pragativadi, Bhubaneswar, Date. 05.09.1999, P. 4.

24. N.R.S. Sexena, op. cit., P. 183.

25. B.C. Naik, op.cit., P. 17.

26. Civil Secretariat Bundle Correspondence, Political 16 of 1865 Nagpur Records, Date. 08.01.1965.

27. Debendra K Dash, and Dipti R. Pattanaik. "Late Nineteenth Century Literary Discourse and Oriya Identity." *Utkal Historical Research Journal.* Bhubaneswar: Utkal University, 2004.

28. Gaganendra N Dash, *Saraswati Fakirmohan: Sahitya O Byaktitwa.* Cuttack: Granthamandir,2006.

29. Nilakantha Dash, *Odia Bhasa O Sahitya.* 1954. Cuttack: New Students Store, 1958.

30. Sarbeswar Dash, *Yugasrasta Fakirmohan.* 1954. Cuttack: Granthamandir, 1983.

31. Sudipta Kaviraj,. *The Unhappy Consciousness: Bankimchandra Chattopadhyay and the Formation of Nationalist Discourse in India.* 1995. New Delhi: OUP,1998.

32. Surendra Mohanty, *Fakirmohan Samikshya.* 1955. Cuttack: New Students Store,1981.

33. Ashis Nandy, *The Intimate Enemy: Loss and Recovery of Self Under Colonialism.*New Delhi: Oxford UP, 1983.

34. Jatin K. Nayak, Ed. *Fakir Mohan Senapati: Perspective on His Fiction.* Jagatsinghpur: Prafulla Pathagar Publications, 2004.

35. Shivarama Padikkal,"Inventing Modernity: The Emergence of the Novel in India." In *Interrogating Modernity: Culture and Colonialism in India.* Tejaswini.

36. Sudhir Niranjana, and V. Dhareshwar, Eds. Calcutta: Seagull Books,1993.

37. Fakirmohan Senapati, *Six Acres and a Third. The Classic Nineteenth-Century Novel about Colonial India.* Translated from Oriya by Rabi Shankar Mishra, Satya.

38. P. Mohanty, Jatindra K. Nayak and Paul St.-Pierre. Introduction. Satya P.

39. U. Mohanty. of California P, 2005.

40. G. Toynbee,. *A Sketch of the History of Orissa.* 1873. Jagatsingpur: Prafulla Publications, 2005.

41. A.K.Warder, *Indian Kavya Literature Vol. III.* 1977. New Delhi: Motilal Banarasi Dass, 1990.

♦♦♦

CHAPTER-VII

EDUCATIONAL IDEAS CONTAINED IN THE LITERATURE OF FAKIR MOHAN SENAPATI

CHAPTER VII

EDUCATIONAL IDEAS CONTAINED IN THE LITERATURE OF FAKIR MOHAN SENAPATI

Fakir Mohan Senapati is more known in the filed of Odia literature than in education. Nevertheless he is one of the greatest teachers of mankind for all time to come. One of the most valuable legacies that he has left to posterity is his educational teaching crystallized in his innumerable literary creations. Though not an educationist in the professional sense of the term, Fakir Mohan Senapati, as a novelist and a philosopher has left us a legacy of thought and ideas that are useful to educators and can give inspiration to young people to shape their personality. He has left us many of the highest ideals of humanity through his beautiful literature and these may be incorporated in education. Fakir Mohan Senapati had deep interest in the field of educational novels, short stories and essays. He made minute observations on the prevalent system of education through his numerous literary creations. Fakir Mohan Senapati's literature contains highly educative values and proves to be a powerful agency of education. His keen interest in the domain of education impelled him to author four exclusive literary works titled Chhamana Athaguntha, Lachhama, Mamu and Prayaschitta.His long narrative novels provide significant implications on the aim of education, curriculum, Women education and role of teachers. Fakir Mohan Senapati's volume of stories titled Sabhya Zamidar, Suna Bahu, and Pathoi Bahu etc. reflects his valuable opinion on vocational education. A reading of Fakir Mohan Senapati's literature reveals many useful educational ideas, which are enlisted in relation to various aspects of education, and are presented in the following paragraphs.

7.1 CONCEPT OF EDUCATION

As has been stated by Fakir Mohan Senapati the process of education has begun since the origin of human civilization and would continue till its existence.[1] Defining the concept of education, he observes that degree or certificate from an educational institution is not the end of education. Education is a continuous process of life. According to him, the whole world is the field of education and the beautiful nature is adequate to educate men. He states that subject of study is unlimited and it includes each and every element in the universe starting from the atoms to the distant planets. The life span of men is too short in comparison to the world of education around him. However the prime duty of a man should be to make life content with whatever education and knowledge he can acquire through the whole span of life.[2]

According to him the heart of the educated is filled with love, respect, devotion and forgiveness. An educated person is always engaged in good work, leads a sacred life in good company and sweet words. He is familiar with important happenings of the past, traditions and customs of different countries, and the rules and regulations of the entire world and always thinks of the development of his region and nation, of course not divorced form the world. He loves literature and serves it. Again Fakir Mohan Senapati argues that all educated persons may not be highly knowledgeable but they must treat knowledge as more precious than the material prosperity. He further notes that an educated person has a heart as high as a mountain and as deep as the ocean.[3]

The announcement of new educational policy was a challenge to Bengali's supremacy in Odisha. In a meeting at Cuttack Debating Society, Rajendralal Mitra pointed out the difficulties of the printing of Odia books and it also hampered the progress of Odisha. In Balasore, Kanti Chandra Bhattacharya wrote a book "Odiaya Swatantra Bhasa Naye". This created a stir among Odia nationalists. Fakir Mohan mobilized public opinion through organizing meetings, Public speeches, writing in Sambad Bahika to challenge such view of Mr.Bhattacharya. A committee was formed by him and some of his friends to save the Odia language. He even prayed to the Odia Amalas in Kacheri to find out the way to save the language. But in fear, they did not come forward to participate in government affairs. The zamindars and the landlords did not dare to start an agitation for this purpose. Once he organized a meeting through uniting the Amalas. He pointed out that "It is not the government order to abolish Odia and to introduce Bengali Language. It is the conspiracy of the Bengalis. All the offices are occupied by them. If Odia is lifted, the Bengalis will become the clerks in the offices. The sons and relatives of the Bengalis will be the amala and the Odia will be driven out from the government offices and will never ever avail any government job.[4]

7.2 AIMS OF EDUCATION

The aims of education are based on the aims of life and these aims of life are reflected in the literature of the time. An evaluation of Fakir Mohan Senapati's literature reveals his perception on the aims and philosophy of life, and thereby provides a general estimation of his concept on the aims of education. Thus Fakir Mohan's aims of education are correlative to his ideals and philosophy of life which is implied in his literature. A discussion on the aims of education reflected in Fakir Mohan Senapati's literature follows.

Fakir Mohan Senapati was an epitome of honesty and integrity. He adopted morality as the ideal of his life and literature. His literature clearly reveals his desire to recrate the society by imparting moral education. Fakir Mohan's deep faith in moral values is reflected in his long novels like Lachhama, Mamu and Prayaschitta, etc and in his short stories like Rebati, Patient Medicine, Sabhya Zamidar, Suna Bahu, Pathoi Bahu, Mauna Mauni etc. These stories provide moral direction to human life and society.

Fakir Mohan Senapati is convinced that the significance of education is in converting a narrow-minded person into a broad-hearted human being by inculcating moral values. In Rebati he emphasizes the role of peers in the formation of character. In another story Mauna mauni, he appeals to the people to fill their hearts with religious qualities through good education. Again in his Dak munsi, Fakir Mohan Senapati argues that true knowledge enable man to attain divinity whereas evil knowledge turns him to a demon.[5]

In his Granthabali, Fakir Mohan Senapati states that education enables one to devote himself to good work and find company with good friends. It fills the heart with Godly qualities like love, respect, devotion, kindness and forgiveness etc. Education enables the individual to avoid bad work and bad companions.[6]

The aforesaid discussion of Fakir Mohan's literature reveals that one of the chief aims of education should be the formation of character by inculcating moral values. This aspect of Fakir Mohan Senapati's educational thought resembles the view of M.K. Gandhi. Gandhiji treated the building of character as an important purpose of education and considered character as the expression of the whole personality including its ethical and spiritual aspect.[7] He attached so much importance to character training that he was prepared to relegate to a subordinate position or even sacrifice literary training if the choice were to be made between the two. Fakir Mohan Senapati believed the same. Fakir Mohan's repeated emphasis on education for moral development can be summarized with the statement of Dr. Radhakumud Mukharjee. [8]

Fakir Mohan Senapati was a man with wide vision and foresight. His literature reveals that education should make man self-dependent. Fakir Mohan, in his short story Balaswari Pangaluna, appealed to the people to be self-dependent. According to him, education is not for the sake of knowledge only; it should also enable man to earn his bread and butter.

Fakir Mohan Senapati himself was a nationalist and believed that education should foster the sprit of nationalism. According to him education should inspire man to work for the improvement of motherland and mother tongue. [9]

This very statement reflects Fakir Mohan Senapati's explicit opinion on the aim of education to foster the spirit of nationalism. Fakir Mohan Senapati has also written many short stories to inspire and motivate Odia people to work for the development of their mother tongue and motherland. In his story Rebati, he gives the clarion call to the people to love and glorify their motherland and mother tongue. His long narrative Chhamana Athaguntha also puts emphasis on fostering the sense of patriotism through the narration of Geography and History of Odisha. He has praised the characters from the chapters of history who have contributed to our national pride and prosperity. In another long novel Lachhama, Fakir Mohan Senapati has tried to develop nationalist spirit in the minds of the people by narrating the heroic deeds and achievement. Again Fakir Mohan Senapati's revolutionary and appealing writings generated great interest among the Odia people to oust the British rulers from the land. Fakir Mohan Senapati, through his literary creations, criticized the oppression caused by the British rulers. By preaching nationalism through the composition of patriotic songs, Fakir Mohan Senapati has made his mind very clear that education should cultivate nationalist sprit. [10]

Fakir Mohan Senapati is considered as a strong advocate of the age old Indian culture and tradition. Through his literature he has tried to preserve and improve the rich Indian culture. Fakir Mohan Senapati's long novels like Mamu, Prayaschitta reveal his intention to cultivate love for Indian culture in developing a sense of love and respect for Indian culture and tradition. Fakir Mohan Senapati reiterates the value of Gurukul education system of ancient India. In Prayaschitta, Fakir Mohan Senapati has tried to glorify the sacred hermitage life of Indian. He has taught Rebati to develop in her the attributes of an ideal woman who adheres to the way and style of living in the line of Indian culture and tradition. In Garudimantra, he has tried to establish people's faith in the moral and religious tradition of India. Fakir Mohan Senapati considers language as an important part of any culture, and through his small poems appeal the people to love, respect and work to maintain the high status and dignity of their mother tongue intact. Thus Fakir Mohan Senapati's literature clearly reveals that cultural aim of education has not been ignored in his implied scheme of education. [11]

7.3. EDUCATION AS AN INSTRUMENT OF SOCIAL CHANGE

Fakir Mohan Senapati was well aware of the social situation of his time. His stories like Beerei Bishala, Daaka Munsi, Sunaa Bahu, Dhulia Baba,Bagala Baguli, Kamalaa Prasad Goraap, Mouna Mouni, Punar Musika Bhaba reflect his desire for social change. Through these stories Fakir Mohan has criticized the social and political exploitation, injustice, rigid casteism, suffering of common men etc. He has also tried to spread the message of peace, friendship and brotherhood in order to give a practical shape to his dream of an ideal human habitation. Fakir Mohan Senapati's attempt to discipline and refine the society by emphasizing on individual human character through provision of ideal society is very clear. [12]

Fakir Mohan Senapati, in his story Suna Bahu, Pathoi Bahu, has emphasized on the vital role that education plays to make one a great man and who does not believe in falsehood, greed and ego. He is truthful, simple and sensitive towards the sorrows and suffering of others. All the novels of Fakir Mohan Senapati very clearly reflect his desire for social reforms; by removing the evils and lacunae of the society. These are satirical novels in which he has criticized the social and political exploitation. The common and innocent people are oppressed by the so called educated elite as well as the ruling class in the name of law, religion and administration. Through his novels he appealed to the people to rise above narrow sectarian and religious attitude and lead a life of peace, prosperity and unity. In his novels Prayaschitta, Fakir Mohan Senapati states that education imparts good knowledge to cultivate divine qualities in man. In his novels Chhamana Athagunthaand Mamu, he stresses on the virtues of a great man, such as, cooperation, sobriety, sacrifice, courage, patience etc. which are necessary to build a healthy society. [13]

Fakir Mohan Senapati has treated education as the backbone of the society. His aim was to bring about a social change using education as the instrument.

Fakir Mohan Senapati was a great humanist, and it was very natural that he wished education to play a vital role in making men nice human beings. According to Fakir Mohan, education should make men sensitive towards human problems. As a humanist, he imagined of a beautiful sublime society above the narrow social feelings. To him, literature is an instrument to educate and enlighten the human society. In his Rebati, Fakir Mohan Senapati has projected Rebati as a forceful character who has exhibited great attributes like patience, perseverance and courage at the time of crisis. It implies that education ought to imbue us with such attributes of humanity. As a great lover of mankind, Fakir Mohan Senapati treats all men equally and considers them to be the children of God.

He glorified humanism and tried to establish the supremacy of human values with the help of powerful characters like Rebati. Fakir Mohan Senapati is considered to be a great poet and novelist. In his works nature is represented in the living form, sharing joys and sorrows of the human world. His articles convey the message of the welfare of humanity while portraying the vicissitudes of life in the world.[14]

Fakir Mohan Senapati's love of man stimulated him to raise the dignity of man by educating him to lead a life, free of exploitation and cut-throat competition, based on the principles of justice, equality, fraternity and religious harmony.

The aforesaid discussion on Fakir Mohan Senapati's views on aims of education depicts that education should bring about a harmonious and integrated development of all aspects of human personality. Because it is the harmoniously developed person that adjusts to his life and environments. According to Fakir Mohan Senapati, education should inspire the individual to realize God, build moral character, ensure livelihood, foster nationalism, preserve and promote the culture and tradition, bring about social changes and above all inculcate great human attributes. By giving so many aims Fakir Mohan Senapati shows his catholicity, his greatness, his breadth of vision, his ability to embrace all aspects of human life.[15]

Fakir Mohan mobilized the Odias and an application with 500 signatures of the Odias was submitted to the Collector John Beams. Collector of Balasore, submitting that "Odia is an ancient language and the teaching is to be given in Odia. As a result the government ordered to lift Bengali language and to establish more schools for the spread of Odia language. From this moment Fakir Mohan began his writing to save Odia language from extinction in the face of the Bengali attack.[16]

The concerted efforts and plans for the development of neighboring Bengali language come to inspire Fakir Mohan's literary career. The main amb was the development of mother tongue. [17]

No one had written short stories like Fakir Mohan : the manner in which he wrote is unique, All the stories are unique in writing style and plot . They all aimed at social reformation. Keeping the social propose in mind Fakir Mohan's stories were created. Fakir Mohan declared war against corruption, injustice and superstition in the society through his stories.

7.4 CURRICULUM AND METHOD OF INSTRUCTION

The philosophy of man on earth determines the aims of education, and curriculum is framed and method of instruction is decided as the means of realizing the aims and objectives of education. Fakir Mohan Senapati advocated high and lofty aims of education, and in order to realize these aims of education he has apparently emphasized on an appropriate curriculum and suitable methods of instruction, which find reflection in his literature.

Fakir Mohan Senapati seems to be in support of a broad and comprehensive curriculum, which is implied in his essay Fakir Mohan Granthavali. In this essay Fakir Mohan states that the whole world is the field of education. The subject of study is unlimited and it includes each and every element in the universe starting from the distant planets to the atoms. The life span of an individual is not sufficient for his education. However, one should be satisfied with whatever education and knowledge one can acquire throughout the life.[18]

Fakir Mohan Senapati emphasizes more on ancient literature than on modern literature. To him, the pleasure of literature makes human life more meaningful, glorified and successful. Fakir Mohan Senapati's Suna Bahu implies that literature can cultivate nationalist spirit in the young pupils, and should form a part of school curriculum. Literature also provides moral education and deep faith in God. Fakir Mohan Senapati's literary creations are full of moral education and give a moral direction to human life and society. Along with literature, grammer also finds a suggested place in Fakir Mohan's framework of curriculum.

Fakir Mohan Senapati also favours religious education to be part and parcel of school curriculum. His desire to impart religious education, especially to women, is reflected in the third canto of his long narrative story Rebati. Thus true education sows the seed of religion in human heart by critically examining it. Fakir Mohan Senapati's concept of religion is not narrow. In his story Adharmabitta, he has made it quite clear that the essence of all religions is humanity.[19]

Social studies get due emphasis in Fakir Mohan Senapati's scheme of education. Fakir Mohan, in his long story Kamalaa Prasad Goraap, Mouna

Mouni, Punar Musika Bhaba, has attempted to foster the sense of patriotism through the narration of geography and history of Odisha. His Rebati is also a historical story.[20]

Though Fakir Mohan Senapati's literature is based on the foundation of ancient ethos and tradition, he himself was very much scientific in temperament and modern in outlook. He advocates that science education should occupy its rightful place in the curriculam. [21]

Fakir Mohan Senapati, in his literature has expressed his intention that education should shape the women as the true representatives of Indian culture and tradition. It should develop necessary skills in the girls so as to enable them to effectively manage the family affairs.

Fakir Mohan Senapati, in his literature, accorded an important place to nature with an aim to educate the people through it. Most of Fakir Mohan's long narratives especially Ajaa Naati Kathaa, Baleswari Rahajani, Pathoi Bahu, Baleswari Panga Luna, Maadha Mohantynka Kanyaa Sunaa, Kaalika Prasad Goraap, Bagala Baguli, Kamalaa Prasad Goraap, Mouna Mouni, Punar Musika Bhaba and many others present nature as beautiful, sensitive and educative as well. [22]

Fakir Mohan, in his literary creations, has projected Nature as a living spirit and has emphasized on the great virtue of nature to educate the human society. Even Fakir Mohan, in his Rebati, tried to develop patriotism through a vivid and comprehensive description of beautiful Odishan nature.[23]

Like Gandhiji, Tagore, Sri Aurobindo and other great Indians, Fakir Mohan also stresses on the importance of mother tongue. His revolutionary writings maintain the high status of the mother tongue and preserve the dignity of the state. Fakir Mohan Senapati considers the fostering of nationalism as an important aim of education, and feels that nationalism not only implies love for motherland, but also love for mother tongue. It is reflected in as many as twenty short stories of his compilations. Again a nation can not develop without proper emphasis on mother tongue.In Fakir Mohan Senapati's opinion, mother tongue as the medium of instruction enables the individual in the free expression of his feelings and foster nationalist spirit as well. Therefore mother tongue should find an important place in the scheme of education. Mother tongue should be the medium of instruction. [24]

Although Fakir Mohan Senapati has not expressed his views exclusively on curriculum and method of instruction, his literature suggests a broad and comprehensive school curriculum. Fakir Mohan Senapati's literature suggests that the school curriculum should include literature, grammer, composition, history, civics, geography, culture, science, vocational subjects like agriculture and diary farming, physical training, aesthetic education, religious education and nature study. Although Fakir Mohan has no where prescribed for a separate curriculum for girls, he has stressed on religious and culture education, and home science to be part and parcel of the curriculum for them. Regarding methods of instruction, Fakir Mohan Senapati's literature suggests very little. However, he emphasizes on mother tongue as medium of instruction, learning while earning, and education through nature as the methods of instruction. [25]

7.5. WOMEN EDUCATION

In ancient Odia literature woman was glorified. Sometimes she was portrayed as a destroyer like Durga and sometimes as a woman who can sacrifice her happiness for her husband like Urmila. Woman was portrayed as such till Independence and by that time she was by nature, shy and submissive. [26]

During the period of Fakir Mohan Senapati, we find woman in a new light. She can be courageous if necessary, and can beat her husband to reform him. But then she also serves him after he is beaten (Patent Medicine). In his works we find two types of woman, traditional and modern. The grandmother of Rebati, the wife of Zamidar is traditional, because they believe in tradition, conventions and superstitions. But there is also Rebati who wants to be educated and modern. [27]

Fakir Mohan Senapati's ideas on women education are truly the reflection of renaissance. Being a male writer, Fakir Mohan Senapati understands the cause of women much better than most writers. The Indian woman is the victim of a terrible conflicting transitional period, torn between two different value systems. In spite of the status of equality bestowed upon her by law, it is difficult for her to change in the core and for the society to free her of the age-old sanskara. Rebati is a teen aged girl of the early part of the nineteenth century who has the quest for knowledge; she is a true renaissance spirit. She was encouraged by her father, mother and teacher Vasu with whom she has a platonic bond of the soul. But as it goes, her grandmother is very much against her education.[28]

Fakir Mohan Senapati is a great social thinker. In the story he portrays the maladies and social taboos like Cholera being treated as a curse from the Goddess and discusses about women education. When the parents and the teacher die of cholera, the old woman blames Rebati's education as an omen for the house. Ultimately both the women die of hunger and poverty. Another character is the wife of Babu Chandramani Pattnaik in the story 'Patent Medicine'. She is at once bold and soft hearted; she knows the responsibilities of the wife. She is intelligent, patient, caring, but unlike the common Odia women, she rises to the occasion and succeeds in bringing a change in her wayward husband by punishing him severely.

Images of woman in Indian literature are characterized by contradiction - there is a conventional image and there is a protesting voice. Post Independence literature reveals the woman's quest for her identity giving rise to a number of issues. The new woman is emerging and there are a number of new themes and issues to be taken in the future. However, two overall views of woman have been dominating Odia literature from ages: the

Sita and the Draupadi archetypes. There is silent suffering with utmost loyalty to man in the Sita type and woman as an individual demanding social justice in the Draupadi type. The later has got greater appreciation. But we have to remember that family plays a pivotal role in the scheme of life. The new woman in Odia literature does not break the family but dreams to make the family "Home Sweet Home". Be it small or big, be it in the courtyard or in the courtroom, woman is the cause of all action. If woman is absent, there is no poetry, no song, no drama, no tears, no laughter and ultimately no life in this world. But they are still walking on a tight rope to accomplish their human rights and social justice.[29]

Odia women at the turn of the century are in the middle phase and the interface of tradition and modernity. Though women writers are tolerant and respectful towards the rich tradition they are still confident of their own new self and sensitive to the dogmatization of traditional values. At the turn of the new millennium Odia literature, as far as the feminist thrust is concerned, is not free from family, history and social modernism. The women in Odia literature are more educated, sophisticated and even rebellious but the woman herself is wary of shedding off the traditional values which forms part of her inherited consciousness.[30]

Women in the rest of Odisha are for the most part still dogma ridden due to lack of education. We have the enlightened brave new woman and we have the helpless, illiterate male-dominated woman existing side by side in life and in literature. The sense of cultural continuity, which serves as the moorings of a society and the writers take their favorite themes like women's education, widow remarriage, abolition of untouchability and freedom. Their writings can become a shared legacy only when there is a process of historical recognition. However, a complex set of processes are there which include the idea of what constitutes a literary tenet, the dominance of a particular kind of discourse and gender biased writings towards oblivious.[31]

Fakir Mohan Senapati, both as a novelist and as an educationist, has accorded an important place to woman, emphasizing on women education. The women are the wealth of the family. They are Goddess of family life. We must develop them with the characters of Rebati.[32]

Fakir Mohan Senapati thought in the same line. He has also realized the role of women in the society as inevitable and has introduced powerful women characters in his literary works. Fakir Mohan Senapati has tried to build up their character with good education. For example in Rebati, Pathoibahu, sunabahu he has emphasised on the women education.

Fakir Mohan has also highlighted on the content of women education in Rebati. Fakir Mohan Senapati's desire to impart religious education to women is very clear in the third canto of the epic.[33] According to Fakir Mohan Senapati, education for women should be designed to make the women aware of the relationship between husband and wife which is based on love, commitment, sacrifice and loyalty so they would lead a good family life. In his epic Sunabahu, Fakir Mohan has conceived the idea of an ideal woman who should be capable of advising and assisting her life partner. She should be endowed with necessary qualities so that she can efficiently play the multi-dimensional role in the society as mother, sister and wife.[34]

Modern education can draw tips from this while planning the content of women education. Fakir Mohan Senapati has projected Rebati as a nice girl who possesses the attributes of ideal Indian womanhood, and completely adheres to Indian way and style of living. According to Fakir Mohan Senapati, character is vital for woman.

A woman needs to extend her fullest cooperation both in personal and professional life of her husband in order to shape his personality. Fakir Mohan Senapati recommends strict code of conduct for women. To him, a woman should not see eye to eye to any male person other than her husband. She should not spend even a moment with any other man. She should refrain from talking in loud voice, and also from making satirical remarks at others.

Further she should pay due regards to the members of her in-law family, especially high respect to mother-in-law and deep love and affection to her sister-in-law.[35] Women should be hospitable, and patient and skilled for the smooth management of family affairs. They should be well trained in preparation of tasty food items. Instead of attaching more importance to dress and attire, woman should develop healthy habits like cleanliness. According to Fakir Mohan Senapati, education should not encourage the modern ladies to forget their duty and social obligation towards their families rather education should make them conscious of their social obligations and traditional role in shaping their family life.[36]

Fakir Mohan Senapati also realized the role and responsibility of woman in the education of their children. He is well aware of the fact that the woman can play a greater role than the man in shaping the personality of the child. Thus Fakir Mohan has stressed on women education so as to validate the saying mother is the first teacher of the child. Finally Fakir Mohan Senapati's views on woman education can be summarized with the statement of Swami Sivananda, who rightly says:

Woman is man's first Guru. And God has fitted her admirably to fulfill this glorious role.

7.6 THE CONTEMPORARY PICTURE OF ODISHA IN FAKIR MOHAN LITERATURE

To start with as like the Sun dispel the darkness prevailing all throughout, the spirit of education dispels the darkness prevailing all thought, the mind, and conscience of human being. The meaning and purpose of Education is very much extensive for a human being. Learning education from birth to death is the only way. In the state of Odisha, consequent upon missionary school and expansion of educational system, educational policy of Macauly, recommendation of commissioner Henry Recat,Rout, Hardiz & declaration of Hardiz as regards service, the education has become vocational oriented. However in practice, as a result of which, education has lost its originality. In Fakir Mohan's literature the same status is observed.

According to Dr. Mayadhara Mansingh's point of view, Fakir Mohan was a born teacher; as such he had got sincere inclination towards education. In Fakir Mohan's literature, information regarding the then non-formal education of primary education, women education, higher secondary education, college education, period of education, principle and directive of beginning of education, courses of study, ecucational equipment & test books & so on so forth are available.

Non-formal Education: - During the childhood period of Fakir Mohan, the system of education was much miserable other than Odias' palm leaves scripture and hand written HARITALI. There was no other source of script, or printed books. Indigenous languages were being found in those days. For general education, teaching was imparted through establishing (Chatsali) non-formal education centre in villages in traditional manner. In this context, Fakir Mohan has stated in his autobiography how the centres were being setup in case of bigger villages, in nearby areas of the town locality. There were personal teachers appointed in economically established families selectively each. Even the untouchable children were also learning along with upper caste children sitting at a distant place.

Abadhana (Teacher) - The teacher of chatsali (Non formal centre) were called Abadhan. The clan belonging to Brahmin, Karan and dynasty of Mati were serving as Abadhana. The teacher belonging to the mati dynasty were called as a OJHA and the other teachers were regarded as APANE.

Rules & discipline at Chatsali- No illegal activites were prevailing at chatsali. Abadhanas (teacher) were the head of the institute. In the absence of Abadhana it was role of Bada Chatas to maintain discipline at chatasali. There were no rights of any disciple without the concern of Abadhana. There was provision of hard-punishment. Such as beating by cane, one footed standing, kneeling down etc. were prevailing. Abadhanas were very much hard-hearted. Even Fakir Mohan himself had experience of bitterness, having been caned mercilessly. All these things are also being clearly mentioned in his story *Randi Pua Ananta*.

Study Materials: - Teaching was imparted on chalk in the morning & books were being taught in the afternoon Session. Out of the text book such as **CHHANDA GRANTHA, BHAGABATA RASA PANCHADHAYEE & MATHURA MANGALA** the teaching of chalk, panikia upto 25 table were contained, **ODANKA, FEDANKA, KADA, GANDA BODI, ODIA** alphabet were also included.

Income of chatsali (Non Formal Centre):- Income of Chatsali through students (Chatas) and donation collected through the students (Chatas).

Educational Equipments:- There were no printed text books other than Bible in Odia. Children were used to write with chalk on the earthen floor, table of multiplication. Alphabets were also being written by the students on the surface through chalks and wood to write on palm leaves as writing equipment. Later on Madhusudan the contemporary of Fakir Mohan were had confronted such situation during his childhood.

Primary Education:- Non-formal education continued for long keeping pace with the modern primary education, as the colonial government could not be able to flourish the spread and propagation of the primary education up to the last year of first half of 19th century up to the level of expectation. The sole architect of 15 numbers of Indigenous Schools which were established during the period of 1922-23, was the missionary. A school was established at Puri in the year of 1835 by the effort and recommendation of the commissioner Willickson, having been advised by the Bengali Educational Committee, However, due to some reason or the other, the institution went collapse in the year February, 1841.The council of education of Bengal which were established in the year 1842 were controlling the school of Odisha. Though before hand as per the decision of

Macaulay's teaching through medium of English the western knowledge and science and the spread of propogation of English literature, were considered to be the ideal, still then eight numbers of schools in Odisha out of proposed 131 schools in the entire country were declared to be taught in Odia medium by Lord Hardiz. Khorda, Puri, Balasore, Remuna, Bhadrak, Kendrapada, Mahanga and Hariharpur were included. During the year 1849-50, only two numbers of linguistic schools such as Mahasinghapur and Khorda were in force. In the year 1849-50, Remuna and Hariharpur had already been closed and in the year 1858-59, Puri and Balasore schools had also been closed. From all these, it is clearly proved that due to lack of teaching method and experienced teachers, teaching education could not be successful.

In his autobiography Fakir Mohan has revealed that more than 40 years ago an English school was set up at Baleswar. Siba Prasad Choudhary, Ganga Prasad Choudhury, Bichitrananda Dash, Atal Bihari Pal, & R. Bengali, these 5 numbers of students were there. Owing to not coming of students due to fear complexities of losing caste identities, indigenous students were reluctant to take admission. As a result of which that English school was closed. The Akborn saheb, while drawing the attention of Chotelal of Bengal, as regards accute backwardness of modern education learned the fact that only in the district of Cuttack & Balaswar 2704 & 839 numbers of Non formal centres respectively, was existent, there upon. Akborn sahib believed that for the speread of moden education, renewal of Non formal centre will be much more fruitful.

Even though much more funds were allotted for the development of education during the tenure of Udesh Despash, still then Odisha was deprived of having been improved upto the expectation level. How ever it was only in the year 1863 the spread of education reached the expectation level in Odisha, when whole hearted ceaseless efforts used by some British employees extending their financial support to the Abadhana (teacher) making payment of students scholarship, establishing teachers training centre formulating text book and printing paying attention for the smooth management of schools. High quality of teaching method appointing qualified teachers was also giving priority to some other determinant factors. In Fakir Mohan's literature, there are numbers of examples more or less reflected on earlier traditional method of teaching in Non formal centres in modern way of primary education, higher education, college education, women education, education of medical doctors and survey education.

The time period of child education of Fakir Mohan began from 1852 and was confined to 1857-58. During that period the educational systems which were flourished all through out the state of Odisha was Non formal education. As per the stastical information during that period only four numbers of modern English school and 25 numbers of vernacular schools were in existence. Out of total of 29 numbers of these schools only, 1046 numbers of students were continuing their education. Fakir Mohan has mentioned in his autobiography about the existence of modern English school in the district of Balasore.

As the text book in Odia **BARNA BODHA, NITI KATHA, TINI BHAGA AND HITOPODESH** were in vogue. As the Bengali text book **SAMBANDHA SARA (PYAR SAHEB), GRAMMAR (KITH), ANKA (KITH)** were prevailing.

In the upper classes in Bengali **KADAMBARI BANGALAR ITIHAS** of Man Sharma, **BHUGOLA AND GANITASARA** were being taught in higher classes in Odia. Apart from this **MISANA, FEDANA, HARANA, GUNANA, NAVIANA, KUTAKRAYA BIKRAYA** etc. Mathematics was being tought. In primary school teaching student regarding the geography of the country, land and abroad were under the juridiction of teaching. During that period Khetratatwa, Barga mula, Bhagnansha, Dasamika, Ghanamula were taken under their responsibility of teaching.

Realising the gravity of the situation of generating sense of nationality of forming separate province of Odisha teachers were engaged themselves reasonably imparting teaching in school devotionally in accordiance with. Thirst for reading of Fakir Mohan was the strong living example of this spirit. Fakir Mohan has depicted a pitiable subtle picture in his piece of verse, title as in Hata Bhahuda.

1854, afterwards education was determined to be the entry card for earning money without being considering as the source of education has been the prime concern.

Secondary education and its area of operation:-

When English education has been economically dependent, at that time appreciation and inclination towards English has been increased considerably. Basing upon this point of view, modern education in addition to the importance of English has been increased. So also it has been easier paving the way of Odia economic development side by side and has been the main concern. In the year 1860 it was observed that Inspector of schools were maintaining much more partiality for Bengal govt. It is clearly apprehended by us in autobiography of Fakir Mohan that second teacher of Balasore English school Babu siba Chandra Some for the spread of education has established Bangotkala(Bangot Utkal), Barabati school despite being in govt. service. For that the concern, the keen interest for higher education of general people have availed utmost development.

Day by day secondary education had gained momentum in spreading of the education. The characters which Fakir Mohan had sketched so far in his literature in between 1842-1880, has vevealed himself as Natabara of the Novel Mamu, Pitambar as persur and zamidar Pratap, Udit Malllah. We could just finalise the development which were occurred during the year 1882-1918 in the novel Prayaschitta and some tales.

Normal school: - Akborn Saheb has experienced for the first time the utility of establishing normal schools & to excute the purpose of that very concept Dr. E.Roi had helped him. As a result, in the year 1868, so as to provide appropriate teacher to the whole mass of school, govt. had approved establishing a large normal school at Cuttack city. An amount of Rs. 1000.00 was sanctioned per month towards the expenditure, there upon20% from each district had registed for undertaking teachers training; Basudeva of Fakir Mohan's story Rebati was the student of normal school. Fakir Mohan himself was also the student of normal school. Arithemetic, Astrology, Physics, and other Science were being taught in those schools. The necessity of trained teacher was increased having been such normal schools and so also there had been a qualitative increase in the field of educational teaching.

Survey school- A proposal was sent to the Govt. in the year 1868 for the arrangement of establishing high school for the teaching of measurement of plot of land. Subsequently in the year 1876, arrangement was made for the opening of a survey school at Cuttack. To register name in that school, one had to pass the minor or a vernacular student will avail the teaching without any payment and will be paid two rupees in the form of scholarship during the study period. Other student will get one rupee fees per month. Tenure of teaching will be two years. During the last four months, the student will learn measuring plot of land, wandering randomly. Having realised the necessity of learning of such education many students registered their name. It is learned from Fakir Mohan's Utkal Brahmana about how much the Ravenshaw Saheb experienced the necessity & utility of such school of survey.

School of Medical Doctor: – In the year of 1877, 15th February Odisha medical school was setup at Cuttack. Primarily it was decided that 20 students will be continuing study making payment of fees & 20 others were allowed to continue their study without any scholarship. It was accepted that the minimum qualification for entering in medical school was fixed as minor pass or vernaculars. Fakir Mohan in his writing Utkal Brahmana has bowed down at the feet of Ravenshaw Saheb & has regrarded him as the founder of general Hospital. Donation from number of benevolent, philanthropic king's emperor, whole hearted administrative aids, advice & good intention so also organizational skill of "Dr Stimoth" had played a predominant role in the advancement of medical school.

Girls School & Women education:-In the modern sense of the term there had been the establishment of the tradition of women education in Odisha, even long before the establishment of girls' school. During the period of Sarala, the example of women education in the page of Mahabharata, in Mahabharata there has been proved different women characters having been charcterised and been reflected. Women were expert in Math, Tantra, Mantra, Astrology and in various field of learning. Delivering the temple of Bhubaneswar and pictures picturised during that period and receiving education of girls, proof of regarding women education in 15th century, one name Madhabi Dash was very much all accredited in Sundhi samaj for her epics and poems. There has been the description of women dance & song. In the anthology of Kalpalata, there has been proving of women protagonist learning music & literature Chata Ichhabati. Even during the period of Kabi Samrat Upendra Bhanja there has been proof of women education. As per his creation Koti Bramhanda Sundari, women were being educated of Khetriya family. The Editor of Utkal Deepika in the year 1881 has remarked having given priority of Child education. For the purpose of establishment of girls education he stated that the tradition of women education is toomuch old. Hence due to some inhuman and baseless vanity and false traditions, blindness and some problems were observed in women education. Even upto the year 1871, there had not been any establishment of school for Hindu girls. Places like Cuttack town, only in that very year of 1871 due to efforts and care of wise gentle men a girl's school was established for the Hindu girls.At first it was run at Abhinash Chandra Chotopadhaya house situated at Balubazar, Cuttack.

Fakir Mohan has illustrated on simile in the Novel Chhamana Atha guntha, having observed usual instinctive shyness of Hindu beauties, like the Hindu brides, bloom at night and during the day time they cover themselves with their petals, out of shyness.

Wife is half life of the husband as such even wife also has got equal rights and responsibilities. Sharada of Fakir Mohan mission school has been described as "Pathama" of Novel Mamu in a gap of few years only. This pathama had taught to Chhand, in Prayaschita Indumati had gained education privately. Some contemporary country girl of Indumati has also received education. In novel Mamu Saraswati Dei is educated so also Chandramani is educated and in Prayaschita Indumati was too educated. But so as to provide inspiration for the smooth management of their school centre was the proper medium of knowledge. The way Fakir Mohan dreamed of woman education during his life time that would enhance the beauty of home, enrich home, sole bestowed with prosperity. He did not like corruption and so more particularly he was strongly against corruption in the name of common education.

College education: - Intermediate of now was called as first Arts few year before the establishment college in the school of cuttack, first Arts class were continuing. Ultimately a college was set up at Cuttack in the year 1876, As a result of serious claim made by the lovers of Education belonging to the district of Cuttack & Balasore. Due to similarity of time period of the establishment of College at Cuttack & upgradation with the time period of incident mentioned in Fakir Mohan's Novel Prayaschitta information regarding the college education of those periods are available.

Astrology:-There was prime importance of education during the period of Fakir Mohan. Being a fatalistic he was dependent upon astrology. The deep concern of astrological sentiment of Fakir Mohan is clearly revealed from the horoscope of Chandramani & its related discussion in his novel Mamu.

Music & Dance:-During the period of Fakir Mohan there were music & dance for recreational purposes. Herewith we confirm the education of dance music of that period.

Study of Medicine:- For the remedy of common diseases, after going through in detail himself, all about the ayurvedic remedy suggested by Charak, Sushruta, Banabhatta & by studing Rasendra sara Sangraha etc., Fakir Mohan could be able to wave out disease of the patient. During that period, modern medical education was not available in the country side. People were bound to keep trust & belief on ayurveda therapy, the evidence in this regard is clearly indicated.

Whole heartedness towards the modern education:-In the field of education in the first half of 19th century, the mindset and mentality of Odias was troublesome. In this period Odia race confronted much more difficulties number of example for the development of modern education are being clearly visible in the literary work of Fakir Mohan. The main character in the Novel Mamu, Dasarathi Das, giving the English education to his two sons Banambar & Natabara & the idea of land law. Baishnaba Charan Pattnaik of Novel Prayschitta, clearly implies the diginified significance of English Education. In the story Rebati the village of people Patapura have acknowledged to get their submission for the establishment of Upper Primary schools in their village. While deputy Inspector of Schools was in tour no suitable school has been set up in appropriate time. In the story of patent medicine, Fakir Mohan has categorically visualized the adverse impact of English education in a subtler way which has been revealed for the readers. First of all Chandramani being a newly educated youth. Secondly the son of land lord has given emphasis to the negative side of English education in comparison to the positive work.

As like Govinda Chandra of Prayaschitta and Madanmohan of Garudimantra had taken admission in the college at Cuttack, landlord Golaplochan though was not so educated had experienced the dignity and significance of study. Accordingly he was too anxious to provide modern education to his belonged son in the story of 'Adharmabitta'. Laxman Mishra has become the Head master, having passed the entrance examination. In the minor school in the story of Dakamunsi the widow one Padma Dei has provided English education to her own children, doing services in other houses. As a result of which Gopal Babu has been able to heart throve of the Muktar.

From all the instances, eagerness towards English education of Fakir Mohan are clearly reflected. Fakir Mohan has illustrated both positive and negative aspect of English education, beautifully before the readers, Having been deprived of Higher education due to scarcity of fund, he has replanted all through out of his life. Therefore he has not committed even a little bit of mistakes, providing higher education to his son. The sympathetic, compassionate feeling towards poor and destitute and ceaseless effort are concerning in the history of education.

While delivering teaching as a teacher, experiencing the acute scarcity of text Books, he has completely devoted himself for writing & composition of Test Books. Realising that the Odia race can survive, only when the Odia language will be flourishing to a greater extent, sustaining its continuity in a full pledged manner. He has been the main protagonist in the field of linguistic revolution, championing the cause, paving the ways of forming a separate Odia Province. Not only that without the strong foundation of 4th pillar of democracy that is press, providing ingredients, generating, sense of freedom spirit among the common masses, it is quite impossible to cherish the vision & dream for the aspiration of the Odia. Accordingly he has constructed a press so as to make available the feedbacks & prerequisites running & publishing news papers, journals & periodical, boosting them to be up to the mark. He has always been concerning for the spread of higher education and, as such demanded the advancement of it and above all he has taken privilege & pride petroniser spirit of championing the cause of wide spread higher education which can ultimately result in formation of a separate odia province. As because he had already learned by heart the backwardness of modern education in Odisha and plight of the then Odia race. Lagging far behind in comparison to many other regions, without caring for any criticism from any corner he would advise the country men to be educated, either of the way and we are enjoying the fruit and flavour of that effort, and as such he deserves salute for ever & ever. Let such soul multiply further & further for the betterment of the soil.

7.7. OTHER ASPECTS OF EDUCATION

In addition to the concept and aims of education, curriculum and methods of instruction, and women education, Fakir Mohan Senapati's literature also reflects important ideas relating to some other aspects of education, which the researcher has come across in course of the critical analysis in literature. They are presented below.

Like M.K.Gandhi, Fakir Mohan Senapati has also advocated free and compulsory education. Accordingly, Fakir Mohan Senapati has not just advocated free and compulsory education, in order to make it a reality he has also stressed on quantitative expansion of education in Odisha.[37]

Fakir Mohan Senapati has put emphasis on child psychology in the process of Education. To him education should be according to the will and interest of the child. He has stressed on mental health. Peace of mind is a necessity for education Concentration in learning is affected by mental stress and strain.

Long since mind has been without exercise, it may gain good results if enabled to get some fertility.

When a flower blossoms its aroma spreads naturally everywhere It is not possible if a half-bloomed flower is made to bloom mechanically.[38]

Fakir Mohan Senapati's contribution is not confined to any specific aspect of education. He has dealt with almost all aspects of education. His educational ideas contain the elements from different philosophical doctrines.[39] Fakir Mohan's emphasis on realization of God and moral development as aims of education affirms his credential as a true champion of idealism. Like a naturalist he considers nature as the best book and argues to impart education through nature.[40] Fakir Mohan Senapati's educational model also contains the flavour of realism. His emphasis on vocational education proves him to be a realist. Again as a pragmatist Fakir Mohan Senapati has tried to relate knowledge to the life of the people. He has also put emphasis on learning while earning. Fakir Mohan's views on education have the imprints of the educational thoughts of the spearheads of educational renaissance in India. Like M. K. Gandhi and Rabidranath Tagore, Fakir Mohan Senapati has emphasized on taking education.[41] Again like M. K. Gandhi, Gopabandhu Das, Gangadhar Meher and many other nationalists of his time, Fakir Mohan Senapati has advocated for free and compulsory education, moral education and vocational training. His emphasis on mother tongue was in tune with many Indian educationalists and political thinkers of his time. To conclude, Fakir Mohan's philosophy of education makes a harmonious blending of different philosophies of education and the thoughts of the great Indian educationists, and is thus, perfectly eclectic in nature. Finally it made a solid contribution to the world of educational thoughts. [42]

REFERENCES

1. M.K.Meher (e.d.) Swabhav Kavi Gangadhar Granthavali, Cuttack : Granthamandir Publication, 1998, P. 321
2. Ibid., P 380
3. J.Panda, "Educational Ideas of Gangadhar Meher", The Educational Review, Vol. CI. No. 10 Madras, October, 1995, PP. 177-178
4. Prafulla Chandra mohanty,Fakir mohan sahityare samakalina Orissa chitra (Oriya).1984.cuttack.p.102.
5. B.C.Naik, Makers of Indian Literature: Fakir Mohan Senapati, New Delhi Shitya Academy, 1996, P. 63
6. Ibid., P.68
7. Ibid., P.72
8. Ibid., P.79
9. V.R. Tneja, Educational Thought and Practice, New Delhi : Sterling Publishers Private Ltd. 1990, P. 190
10. K.Bhatia and B.Bhatia, The Philosophical and sociological Foundation of Education, New Delhi: Doaba House,1991, P. 77
11. B.N.Dash, Principles of Education and Education in the Emerging Indian Society, New Delhi : Ajanta Publication , 1982, PP. 104 and 109
12. J.Panda, "Philosophical Doctrines of Gandhi and Gangadhar : A comparative view", Global Peace, Vol. No. 2, Meerut, December, 2001, PP. 33-35
13. A.K.Choudhury, "Gangadhar: The Kalidas of Oriya Literature", Folk Festival Suvemir, Sambalpur. 2004. PP. 157-159

14. S.Mahapatra. Meher Sahityare yuga Chetana, Cuttack : Students Store 1986 PP. 187-189

15. B.K.Nayak, Education in Emerging Indian Society, Berhampur : Taratarini Pustakalaya, 1999, P. 214

16. N.Pradhan, P.C.dash and P.K.Mahapatra, Principles of Education, Cuttack : Modern Publishers, 2003, P. 142

17. Swami Sivananda, Religious Education, Sivanandanagar : The Divine Life Society, 1970, P. 45

18. Natabar Samantaray, Oriya Sahitvara itihas, (Oriya) 1964, Bhubaneswar p.285

19. Mayadhar Mansingh, Saraswati Fakir Mohan (Oriya) ,1981 Cuttack p.20.

20. P.C. Mohanty (ed), Senapati Sahityaloka (Oriya),1989 Balasore,p .168

21. Sambad Bahika, 22 November 1877.

22. Ibid 7January 1878

23. Ibid. 1 January 1875

    Natabar Samantaray Vyasabi Fakir Mohan (Oriyas). 1957 Cuttack pp. 58-59

24. Braja Mohan Mohanty, Adhunika Oriya Sahitya (Oriya) 1963 Cuttack, p. 51

25. Surendra Mohanty, Oriya Sahityara Kramabisaka (Oriya), 1963 Cuttack p.35.

26. M.N. Das (ed), Side Lights on History and Culture of Orissa. 1977, Cuttack p. 415.

27. Srinibas Mishra , Adhunika Oriya Gadhya Sahitya (Oriya) 1978 Cuttack p. 153.

28. B.C. Samal, Oriya Galpa Srasta Manas Part 1 (Oriya), 1978 Cuttack pp 9-11.

29. Golak Chandra Mohapatra, op.cit.p.39

30. B.C . Samal ,op.cit.pp.16-21

31. Khageswar Mohapatra, op.cit.pp.913-914

32. B.C.Acharya, Oriya Sahityara Sankhipta Parichaya (Oriya). 1977. Cuttack p.217

33. Khageswar Mohapatra, op.cit. p.615

34. Surendra Mohanty, Fakir Mohan Samikshya (Oriya) , 1972 Cuttack pp. 27-29.

35. Fakir Mohan Senapati ,op.cit.pp.92-94.

36. Surendra Mohanty, Fakir Mohan samikshya (oriya),1972.cuttack,p.9.

37. Pratulla Chandra Mohanty ,op.cit,p.26.

38. Ibid,p.29.

39. Laxmi Narayan Sahu, Parolokagata Kabi Fakir Mohan, Utkala Sahitya (Oriya), Part-22, 4th number, Srabana,P.123

40. Ibid..p.163.

41. Natabar Samantaray,Vyasakadi fakir mohan (oriya) 1972. Bhubaneswar. P.50.

♦♦♦

CHAPTER-VIII

SUMMARY, CONCLUSION AND RECOMMENDATIONS FOR FURTHER STUDIES

CHAPTER VIII
SUMMARY, CONCLUSION AND RECOMMENDATION FOR FURTHER STUDIES

8.1 SUMMARY

8.1.1 RESTATEMENT OF THE PROBLEM

In the later part of 19th century four great contemporary Odia litterateurs, namely, Radhanath Rai, Madhusudan Rao, Gangadhar Meher and Fakir Mohan Senapati played a commendable role not only for the upliftment and enrichment of Odia language and literature but also for the thoughts and ideas contributed to the field of education. Radhanath Rai and Madhusudan Rao were working in the field of education in different capacities and they deliberately and practically contributed to education. Fakir Mohan Senapati and Gangadhar Meher were not directly associated with the education of the time. However their contribution to the field of education can not be ignored. The educational ideas contained in their literature are of high relevance and significance in the present educational context. A number of researches have been conducted to study the educational contributions of Radhanath Rai, Madhusudan Rao and Fakir Mohan Senapati, but so far no substantial research work has been conducted to evaluate the educational ideas present in the literature of Fakir Mohan Senapati. Moreover, the literature of Fakir Mohan Senapati contains invaluable philosophical educational ideas, which need to be studied in proper perspectives. Hence the present study:

EDUCATIONAL VALUES AND IDEAS CONTAINED IN THE LITERATURE OF FAKIR MOHAN SENAPATI

8.1.2. OBJECTIVES OF THE STUDY

The objectives of the present study are stated as follows:-

i) To give an outline of Odisha during the time of Fakir Mohan Senapati (physical features, political scenario, social system, economic condition, cultural background and public instruction)

ii) To give a brief life sketch and philosophy of Fakir Mohan Senapati.

iii) To give a brief description of the literary works of Fakir Mohan Senapati so as to study the educational ideas contained in his literature with relation to :

- Concept of education
- Aims of education
- Curriculum and method of instruction
- Women education

8.1.3. METHODOLOGY

The researcher adopted source analytic method based on intensive library research and critical analysis of the themes of the works of Fakir Mohan Senapati. Materials were collected from both primary and secondary sources. The relevant literature of Fakir Mohan Senapati, his letters and correspondences, various official records, reports of committees and commissions relating to education, and gazetteers were taken as primary sources of data. Other sources like books. Journals, periodicals, newspapers, literary criticisms, and published and unpublished research work, records from the achieves of Odisha were consulted. The collection data were carefully and critically studied and discussed on the basis of the set objectives.

8.1.4 CHAPTER WISE SUMMARY OF THE STUDY (CHAPTER III TO VII)

The whole study has been divided into eight chapters.

- Chapter **I** introduce the problem consisting of the relationship between literature and education, need and title of the study, scope and delimitation, objectives of the study and methodology.
- Chapter **II** reviews the related literature available in the field.
- Chapter **III** Odisha during the time of Fakir Mohan Senapati deals with Physical Features, Political Scenario, Social System, Economic Condition, Cultural Backgrounds, Public Instruction, Indigenous Education and Western Education.
- Chapter **IV** Life Sketch of Fakir Mohan Senapati deals with the Family Background, Birthplace, Childhood, Education, Profession, Fakir Mohan as Teacher, Fakir Mohan as Journalist, Fakir Mohan as a social Reformer, Fakir Mohan as an Administrator, Family life, Poverty, Character.
- Chapter **V** Literary works of Fakir Mohan Senapati deals with his different novels and short stories.
- Chapter **VI** Fakir Mohan's Philosophy of life deals with Fakir Mohan a Believer in God, a Staunch Idealist, a Lover of Nature, a Humanist and a Nationalist.
- Chapter **VII** Educational ideas contained in the literature of Fakir Mohan Senapati deals with the Concept of Education, Aims of Education, Education as an instrument of social change, Curriculum and Method of Instruction, Women Education, The contemporary picture of Odisha in Fakir Mohan's literature and other aspects of Education.

A chapter wise summary form Chapter III to chapter VII is presented here under.

8.1.4.1. CHAPTER III: ODISHA DURING THE TIME OF FAKIR MOHAN SENAPATI

Odisha during the time of Fakir Mohan Senapati was passing through a critical period. It was a name usually given to the geographical area in which the Odia speaking people occupied a dominant place. Its territorial boundary was limited to Odisha division of the Bengal presidency. Odisha encompassed two geographical regions, namely, the coastal plains and the highlands featured by hills and forests. A frequent natural calamity was the other indispensable factor of the physical design of Odisha.

During this period Odisha was placed under several administrative jurisdictions, viz (i) Bengal and its Orissa division, (ii) Chhotnagpur, (iii) the Central Provinces, (iv) Madras, and (v) the feudatory states of Odisha. The period was marked by the growth of political awareness and unity among the Odia speaking people, the creation of the province of Bihar and Odisha in 1912. The movement of a separate Odisha province under the stewardship of Utkal Union Conference, and the whole hearted participation of Odia speaking people in the national movement for freedom are considered as the milestones in the political scenario during the time.

Odisha also witnessed institutional decay in its social system during the period. The people were simple, conservative, superstitious, dogmatic and devoutly religious and priest ridden. There was severe social exploitations by the Zamindars, and petty officials and clerks under the government. However, the social reforms like the abolition of Sati and child marriage, promotion of women education, suppression of Meriah and infanticide, construction of roads and establishment of schools resulted in the manifold changes in the social life of the people. The rigorous caste system was whittled down by mass participation in the national freedom movement.

During the period, the economy of Odisha was thoroughly deranged due to frequent droughts and floods, over dependence on agriculture, faulty and revenue administration, lack of communication, non-utilization of natural resources and above all, misgovernance and the rapacious attitude of the rulers.

The culture of Odisha was identified with the all embracing Jagannath culture. It was highly enriched by the Odishan and Chauhan style of architecture. Odisi dance and the dances and songs of tribal dominating western region of Odisha significantly enriched the native culture. The period was marked by renaissance of Odia literature, introduction of printing press, wide circulation of newspapers and books, and the role of journalism in ushering a new age of awakening in Odisha.

During the time of Fakir Mohan Senapati both indigenous and western education continued to co-exist in Odisha. There was declining trend in the position of indigenous education due to the inroad and gradual expansion of western education. However, the progress of education in general was much slower in the western hilly region of Odisha as compared to that in the coastal plains. Fakir Mohan Senapati's own education was limited to the scope of indigenous education up to class V in spite of the facilities for western education in the state.

8.1.4.2. CHAPTER IV LIFE SKETCH OF FAKIR MOHAN SENAPATI

Fakir Mohan Senapati was born on Friday, the 14th of January 1843 or 1250 of the Sana era in the village of Malikashpur in Balasore. His father was Laxman Charan Senapali and mother, Tulsi Dei.

After the death of his parents, he was brought up by his grandmother, Kochila Dei. The role of father and mother was played by his uncle Porusattam Senapati and his grandmother respectively. Till the age of eight he had to suffer this irrevocable agony. During that period, his grandmother saved his life from death. In order to cure him she called two Muslim piras of Balasore. She made a vow before them that "after the recovery of my child Braja, I will make him your Fakir," "Fakir" (Muslim mendicant). Miraculously, the boy originally named Braja Mohan recovered and became known as Fakir Mohan.

The name Fakir Mohan itself implies the fusion of both Muslim and Hindu communities. Besides that, his life is also a glaring example of Muslim impact on Hindu culture.

At the age of nine Fakir Mohan received his early education in the village school. The time when he entered the school, there was neither any printing press nor text books nor were there writers and readers. Even the existence of Odia as a language was being doubted and questioned by people at the helm of educational affairs.

Fakir Mohan secretly obtained admission in the Mission School at Barabati of Balasore town. There he studied history, geography and mathematics. He impressed his teachers with his talent. But he discontinued his education there because he was unable to pay only 25 paise per month as the school fees.

Fakir Mohan was admitted into Barabati School of Balasore. In the examination at the end of the year Fakir Mohan came to top and was promoted. Then the school secretary, Babu Sivachandra Soma, gave him the post of third teacher on the monthly salary of only two and half rupees.

John Beams getting well acquainted with Fakir Mohan's calibre insisted him to be the "Diwan" of Nilagiri. He served as the Diwan of Nilagiri from 1871 to 1875 at a monthly salary of Rs. 1, 000/- after which he served as "Diwan" at various places of Odisha. He was Diwan at Damapada from 1876 to 1877, at Dhenkanal from 1877 to 1883, at Daspalla from 1884 to 1886, at Pallahada from 1886 to 1887, at Keonjhar from 1887 to 1892, at

Damapada for the second time from 1894 to 1896. He stayed at Cuttack from 1896 to 1905 and was attached with various institutions of literature. He spent his last time at Balasore till death.

8.1.4.3. CHAPTER V LITERARY WORKS OF FAKIR MOHAN SENAPATI

"When there is the bustle of progress everywhere, will Utkal be still in slumber?" This line from Fakir Mohan's first original poem *Utkal Bhraman* (Tours of Orissa) not only epitomises his literary overview but also depicts his flare for Odia nationalism. Fakir Mohan Senapati, regarded as the father of modern Odia literature, dedicated his entire life for the progress of Odia language. He also played a leading role in establishing the distinct identity of Odia language and literature. So the story of Fakir Mohan is indeed the story of the "renaissance" in Oriya literature.

Unlike his predecessors, Fakir Mohan completely discarded the traditional theme of romantic love between prince-princess and wrote about common people and their problems in his novels. In contrast to the Sanskritised style of his contemporaries, he also used colloquial idiomatic Oriya in his writings with great skill and competence. If the works of earlier novelists seemed like prose renderings of medieval *kavyas*, Fakir Mohan's novels were realistic to the core. Fakir Mohan can be favorably compared with twentieth century novelists like Premchand and Bibhutibhusan Banerjee.

Fakir Mohan's autobiography "*Atma Jiban Charita*" is not only the first of its kind in Odia but remains the best and most interesting in India languages. Moreover, it is as readable as any of his novels and exciting short-stories. *Vyasa Kavi's* novels are *Chhamana Athaguntha* (1902), *Lachhama* (1903), *Mamu* (1913) and *Prayaschita* (1915). *Lachhama* is a historical novel set against the backdrop of Maratha invasion of Odisha in the eighteenth century. The other three novels are portraits of contemporary society of Odisha. All these four novels depict the social history of Odisha from the eighteenth to early twentieth century.

Lachhama is a story of the Maratha invasion of Odisha which depicts the suffering and the heroic resistance of an Odia country girl in the face of invasion. "*Chha Mana Atha Guntha*" is a vivid account of the exploitation of poor village folk by *Zamindars. Mamu*, again is a story of exploitation of village folk by petty government officials and clerks "*Prayaschita*" potrays the predicament of a semi-educated youth who persistently defies the old order of things with an over enthusiasm for new western values.

Exploitation of the poor villagers by *Zamindars* and the rise of a new class of exploiters among the petty officials and clerks under the British Government were the two dominant traits of ninteenth century Odisha's social history and Fakir Mohan chose to write about them in "*Chha Mana Atha Guntha* and *Mamu*. In this novel he studied the conflict between traditional Indian values and western values as understood by the educated youth of the time, which clearly suggests that he was neither a traditionalist nor an over-zealous advocate for the new wave of westernization that was sweeping the country during his time.

Exploitation of the poor by the rich was a dominant theme in Indian fiction, especially in the Thirties and Forties. Fakir Mohan is perhaps the first Indian novelist to write about it, thus anticipating works like Premchand's "*Godan*". Though Fakir Mohan was almost a contemporary of the great Bengali novelist Bankim Chandra Chatterjee, he was surprisingly different from Chatterjee about the choice of theme as well as language and style. Fakir Mohan's colloquial style is in sharp contrast to Chatterjee's high flown Sanskritised prose.

Fakir Mohan's sense of humour and irony has remained unsurpassed in Odia literature and it is his characteristic style which made him popular with a wide range of readers. He believed that Faith, Asceticism, Love and Devotion were four pillars that formed the base of '*Dharma*'. His faith was derived from Islam, asceticism from Buddhism, love from Christianity and devotion from Vaishnavism.

8.1.4.4. CHAPTER VI: FAKIR MOHAN SENAPATI'S PHOLOSOPHY OF LIFE

Fakir Mohan Senapati's Literary creations, experiences of life and correspondence with the contemporaries reveal his philosophy of life. His philosophy is deep-rooted in Indian idealism and spiritualism.

Fakir Mohan Senapati was a believer in God. He believed God as the ultimate reality and surrendered his ego to Him. He regarded God as the universal soul. Fakir Mohan Senapati emphasized on devotion and self-less dedication to humanity to realize God.

Idealism formed the base of Fakir Mohan Senapati's life and literature. As an idealist Fakir Mohan Senapati led a life based on simple living and high thinking. He believed in certain ideals and principles, and lived to uphold and glorify those ideals. Even he selected contents and characters of his literature that could help in establishing truth and ideals in the society. His literature never entertained any negative aspect of life like nudity and moral indiscipline. Further he was, endowed with moral virtues, and accorded more significance to virtues than wealth. Like a champion of idealism, he believed in the three absolute values of life-truth, beauty and goodness.

Fakir Mohan Senapati was a strong lover of nature. He personified Nature by injecting life into it and emphasized on the great virtue of educating human society through nature. In Fakir Mohan Senapati's subtle vision, Nature is always sympathetic to human cause. According to him, nature is a tested friend and solace giver, and equally shares human emotions like sorrows and happiness. Fakir Mohan Senapati's treatment of nature emphasized more on the internal nature of man than the external physical objects. Fakir Mohan Senapati's subtle vision discovered a harmony between man, nature and God. Fakir Mohan Senapati treated Nature as the best book. According to him, the whole world is the field of education, and Nature is sufficient to educate man.

Fakir Mohan was a great humanist. Through his innumerable literary creations he tried to inform, educate and enlighten people about the noble virtues of humanism. He believed in the fatherhood of God and brotherhood of man. Fakir Mohan's creations reflect his desire for a human society based on justice, equality, fraternity, secularism and other democratic principles. He voiced his resentment against exploitation of innocent illiterate and rural masses. Fakir Mohan Senapati believed in only one religion i.e. human religion.

Fakir Mohan Senapati composed short stories and novels to inculcate nationalist sprit in the people. He appealed the people for a wholehearted devotion to motherland and mother tongue. As a nationalist, Fakir Mohan played an active role in the movement to establish Odia as an independent language and Odisha as separate province. Although Fakir Mohan Senapati did not take active part in the national freedom struggle of India, his contribution was not negligible. His revolutionary and appealing writings influenced the people to fight to oust the foreign rulers from the land. His nationalism was also not opposed to internationalism.

8.1.4.5 CHAPTER VII: EDUCATIONAL IDEAS CONTAINED IN THE LITERATURE OF FAKIR MOHAN SENAPATI

Although not an educationist himself, Fakir Mohan Senapati has thrown light on various aspects of education through his vast literary works. His views on the concept of education, aims of education, curriculum, methodology, teacher-taught relationship, women education, free and compulsory education, and adult education are worth mentioning.

Fakir Mohan Senapati has defined education as life long process. Education does not end in school. He has treated the whole world as the field of education and nature as the daily resettable volume. According to him education refines the feelings of heart. Fakir Mohan Senapati has categorized people into three groups; educated, uneducated and pseudo-educated. The heart of an educated person is filled with love, respect, devotion and forgiveness. He is always engaged in good work and leads his life in good company and sweet words. Such a person believes in God, loves literature and considers knowledge more precious than material prosperity. Fakir Mohan Senapati has compared an uneducated person with the best who always whiles away his time with bad company and in condemnable activities. Fakir Mohan Senapati has termed the third category of people as pseudo-educated. Such an individual pretends to be educated but is not so in true sense of the term. His heart is filled with cruelty, falsehood and other such complexities. A pseudo-educated considers a degree or a certificate from an educational institution as the end of education. Luxurious life style, costly attire, proud of using foreign tongue, and feasting with meat and wine are considered by him as symbols of a civilized life.

Fakir Mohan Senapati's aims of education are correlative to his ideals and philosophy of life, and are reflected in his literature. According to him education should inspire the individual to realized God, build moral character, ensure livelihood through vocational training, foster the sprit of nationalism and above all inculcate great human attributes. In addition to that he has also emphasized on physical development. However Fakir Mohan Senapati considered realization of God as the aim of life and education.

Although Fakir Mohan Senapati has not expressed his views exclusively on curriculum and methods of instruction, his literature suggests a broad and comprehensive school curriculum, Fakir Mohan Senapati's literature suggests that the school curriculum should include literature, grammar, composition, history, civics, geography, culture, science, vocational subject like agriculture and dairy farming, physical training, aesthetic education, religious education and nature study. Although Fakir Mohan Senapati has nowhere prescribed for a separate curriculum for girls, he has stressed on religious and cultural education and home science to be part and parcel of the curriculum for them. Regarding method of instruction, Fakir Mohan Senapati's literature suggests very little. However, he has emphasized on mother tongue as medium of instruction and learning.

Fakir Mohan Senapati has realized the role of women in the society as inevitable, and has introduced powerful women characters in his literary works. He has tried to build up their characters with good education. He was in favour of the spread women education based on Indian culture. His literature suggests that religious education, moral education, discipline, lesson on management of family affairs and upbringing of children and home science to be the content of women education.

Fakir Mohan Senapati's literature reflects his view in favour of free and compulsory education. In order to make it a reality, Fakir Mohan Senapati has stressed on quantitative expansion of education. He has also advocated for adult education to provide functional literacy to the illiterate peasants. He has appealed to them to work in the day and learn in the night. Fakir Mohan Senapati has put emphasis on child psychology in the process of education. Education should be according to the will and interest of the child. He has also stressed on mental health. Concentration in learning is affected by mental stress and strain. He has also emphasized on the need of motivation in the process of education, and has considered reward as a necessary factor for motivation in learning.

Fakir Mohan Senapati's philosophy of education not only makes a harmonious blending of different philosophy of education, but also has the imprints of the thoughts of the great Indian educationists who have brought fresh light in the field of education.

8.2. CONCLUSION

Fakir Mohan Senapati was born at a time, which coincided with the dismemberment of his home district from Odisha division and annexation of the same to the Central provinces. He was born in a poverty stricken family in a remote village. His family environment was not learning friendly. In spite of all these odds, Fakir Mohan Senapati introduced himself to the vast Sanskrit literature of the time, which was instrumental in unfolding his potentiality.

Fakir Mohan Senapati himself had limited education. He was neither an educationist like the two contemporaries Radhanath Rai and Madhusudan Rao, nor did he try formally to intervene in the system of education of the time. Both Radhanath Rai and Madhusudan Rao, in their capacities as teachers and officers of education department, had many textbooks to their credit to rescue the identity of Odia speaking people. Although some of Fakir Mohan's stories and novels had been selected for their textual content of the time, he had not created them objectively for a text. Never the less, Fakir Mohan's vast literature presents a critical appreciation of the highly rich Indian tradition and customs. The protagonists of his long narratives demonstrate living examples of the do's and don'ts of social virtues. The numerous educational ideas present in the literature of Fakir Mohan constitute a major source of informal mass education. It is quite common among the masses in Odisha that they do not forget to quote some educative lines from the popular Odia writters to help solve social discord and to explain and establish their arguments in social situations. This socio-linguistic skill is not limited to the literates only. Thus Fakir Mohan Senapati occupies the first position among his equals due to the oriental inclination of his characters in nourishing a tradition of informal education.

As presented in the foregoing summary Fakir Mohan Senapati believed that God and nature are undivided and the same. He could realize God through nature, and nature through the virtues of humanity. Nature and God should be the foundation of any idealistic frame of education. The rich cultural heritage of India including its religions, sects, traditions, and customs are by nature idealistic. It may be befitting to note that any plan of education, long or short, should not lose sight of this inherent idealistic vision of India. At present we are living in a globalized society, moving faster towards an unhealthily competitive liberalized economy, and a highly vested and privatized world of knowledge. Even while pursuing the same due to political compulsions, it would be perilous on our part to leave behind our roots. It is an emergent need now than ever before to explore a selective bond between ideailism and materialism.

His short stories Rebati cross the borders of time and space in delineating the teacher taught relationship. The lines from the story should be the guiding principles for a teacher anywhere on earth. They carry universal message. A teacher can be reminded of his sacred duty through these short liners by writing them on the school walls. Similarly this is capable of communicating the most comprehensive and broader concept of education. His essays have all the qualities to be included in the language and literary text of any teacher-training programme. The personal letters written by Fakir Mohan to his friends and relatives are also equally rich. They carry the indelible imprint of the novelist, his educationalist philosophy of life, which are value packed. They not only portray the writer's character but also of those great personalities to whom the letters have been written. Selection of such letters in the school language and literature text will not only teach humble ways of letter writing, it will also instill the noble virtues of the personalities in the young learners.

It has been outlined above that Fakir Mohan Senapati was not highly educated nor an official working in the department of education. Obviously he has not given anything purposefully to construct a curriculum. The methods of instruction have not been exclusively spelt out. Like any other idealistic thinker, Fakir Mohan Senapati has contributed more to enrich the aims of education than the curriculum or the methods of instruction. However, glorification of the mother tongue and motherland gets priority in Fakir Mohan Senapati's consideration which seems relevant today. The educational ideas, which are inclusive in his vast literature, can prepare the foundation of a system of informal education. So are the ideas, which are exclusive in nature, can enrich the formal system of education. It is needless to say that the educative lines from Fakir Mohan Senapati's literature should draw the attention of the curriculum framers and policy planners in the field of education in Odisha.

8.3. RECOMMENDATIONS FOR FURTHER STUDY

The present study is a modest and humble attempt of literary analysis in the field of education. It was limited to studying the published works of Fakir Mohan Senapati and outlining the educational ideas contained in his literature. The researcher has refrained from searching his unpublished works. However, they are not traceable till date.

Fakir Mohan Senapati's personal letters to his friends and family members have been published. During the course of this study the researcher found that the personal letters focus directly on the personality of Fakir Mohan Senapati. The same is true in case of the letters written by other renowned personalities of Odisha to Fakir Mohan Senapati. However all such letters by such personalities will definitely throw light on the education system of the time and the educational philosophy of these personalities who were in the forefront in shaping the language and education of the time.

In addition to that studies as given below, may be taken up by the future researches.

A comparative study of educational contributions of Gangadhar Meher, Radhanath Rai and Madhusudan Rao.

A comparative study of humanitarian education in the work of Fakir Mohan Senapati and poet Bhima Bhoi.

Educational movement at Satyavadi; The contributions of Panchasakha.

A comparative study of the idealistic concepts in the literary works of two great personalities of Odisha Radhanath Rai and Fakir Mohan Senapati

♦♦♦

BIBLIOGRAPHY

BIBLIOGRAPHY

Adhikari, P., (ed), (1981) Ama Jagannatha Ama Sanskruti. Cuttack

Behuria,N.C., (ed), (1990) Orissa State Gazetteer, Vol.I, Government of Orissa.

Bhatia, K., and Bhatia, B.,(1991).The Philosophical and Sociological Foundation of Education, New Delhi : Boaba House

Bhattacharya, P., (1980) Maa Evevi Achhanti (translated into Oriya by Jayanti Rai), Jajpur : Matrusadan

Biswal, C., (1989). A Study of the Contribution of Radhanath Rai and Madhusudan Rao in the 19th Century Educational Situation in Orissa, Unpublished Ph.D Thesis, Sambulpur University

Boulton, J.V., (1993). Phakirmohan Senapati : His life and Prose fictions, Bhubaneswar : Orissa Sahitya Acadmy

--------------- (1979). Second Survey of Research in Education (1972-1978), Baroda : Society of Educational Research and Development

----------------- (1986) Third Survey of Resarch in Education (1978-1983), New Delhi : NCERT

-----------------(1991) Fourth Survey of Research in Education (1983-1988) Vol-1, New Delhi : NCERT

Buch, M.B., (ed), (1974) A Survey of Research in Education. Baroda : CASE

Chaube, S.P., (1967) Recent Philosophies in India, Agre : Ram Prasad and Sons, Publishers

Das, B.N., (1982) Principles of Education and Education in Emerging Indian Society, Delhi : Ajanta Publication.

Das, C.R., (1982) A Galimpse into Oriya Literature, Bhubaneswar: Orissa Sahitya Academy

Dubois, A.J.A., (1953) Hindu Manners, Customs and Ceremonies, Oxford.

Dwivedia., P.K., (1998) "Gadysilpi Gangadhar", The Weekly Samaj, Vol 79, 41 Cuttack, August 8. PP. 19.2

Gupta, G.R., (1983) Religion in Modern India, New Delhi

Hamitaon, W., (1812) A Geographical Statistical and Historical Description of Hindustan and its adjacent countries, Vol. II. London

Honby, A.S. (2000) Advanced Learner's Dictionary of Current English. Oxford University Press.

Hunter, W.W., (1872) Orissa, Vol. II London

Kopf, D., (1969) British Orientation and Bengal Renaissance, Calcutta.

Kothari, C.R., (1990) Research Methodology: Methods and Techniques, New Delhi : Wiley Eastern Limited

Mahapatra, B., (1976) Odia Andolanara Itihas, Cuttack

Mahapatra, B.P., (1997) Matrubhasa Odia, Cuttack : Friends Publishers

Mahapatra, P.K., (2003) Principles of Education, Cuttack: Modern Publishers

Mahapatra, S., (1986) Meher Sahityara Yugachetana, Cuttack: Students Store Publication

Manshingh, M, (1962) History of Oriya Literature, New Delhi: Sahitya Academy

Mansing, M., (1967) Odiya Sahityara Itihasa, Cuttack: Granthamandir Publication.

Meher, B., (1977) Pitru Prasanga, Cuttack : Orissa Book Store

Meher, K.C., (1979) Anka O Ankura, Cuttack : Orissa Book Store

Meher, M.K.,(e.d)(1994) Swabhav Kavi Gangadhar Granthavali, Cuttack: Granthamandir Publication

Mohanty, P. C., (1998)Sahityara Samvidhana, Sambalpur: Saraswata Book Store.

Mohanty. J., (1993) Children,s Literature of Orissa, Bhubaneswar : Sahitya Academy

Mukharjee, P., (1964) History of Orissa, Vol, Utkal University

Naik, B.C., (1996)Makers of Indian Literature : Fakir Mohan Senapati, New Delhi : Sahitya Academy

Nanda, B.K., (1995) "Sahitya O Samaja", The Samaj, Cuttack, Febrauary 2, P. 7

Nanda, F.B., (1998) "Gyanayogi Sri Sudhal Dev", The Samaj, October 4, P. 7

Nanda, S., (1979) Coalition Politics in Orissa, New Delhi : Sterling Publication Ltd.

Nayak B.K., (1999) Education in the Emerging Indian Society, Berhampur : Taratarini Pustakalaya

NECRT (2000) Fifth Survey of Research in Education (1988-1992), Vol II, New Delhi : NCERT

O' Malley, L.S.S.,(1917) Bengal, Bihar and Orissa, SikKimm, Cambridge

Panda, J, (2001) Philosophical Doctorines of Gandhi and Gangadhar : A comparative view, Global Peace, Vol. I, No. 2, Meerut, December, PP 33-35

Panda, J., (1996) Moral Education in the Literature of Gangadhar Meher, Orissa Review, Vol. LIII. No. 1, Bhubaneswar, Agust. PP. 12-13

Panda, j., (1998) Gangadhar Meher : A Nationalist, Orissa Review, Vol. LV, No. 1, Bhubaneswar August, PP. 17-18

Panda, P.C., (1894) British Administration in Orissa (1912-1936), New Delhi : Inter India Publication

Pati, M.S., (1992) Circumference and Centre : An Enquiry into Gangadhar's Poetic Matrix, West Orissa: A Study in Ethos., Sambalpur University

Pati., M.S, (1994) Makers of Indian Literature : Gourishankar Ray, Bhubaneswar : Orissa Sahitya Academy

Pati., M.S, (1994) Makers of Indian Literature : Gourishankar Roy, Bhubaneswar : Orissa Sahitya Academy

Pati., M.S., (1992) Circumference and Centre : An Enquiry into Gangadhar's Poetic Matrix, West Orissa : A Study in Ethos., Sambalpur University.

Patnaik, N.R., (1989) Social History of 19th Century Orissa, Allahabad

Patra, P.K., (1943) Odissare Baptist Missionary Societyra Karya Baptist Mission Press.

Patra, S.C., (1979) Formation of the Province of Orissa, Calcutta.

Pradhan N, Dash P.C.,and

Roadman, W., B., and

Ross, J.S., (1942) Ground Work of Educational Theory, London : George G, Harrap & Co. Ltd.

Samantray., N., (1964) Odia Sahityara Itihas, Cuttack

Samantray., R.C.(1998) "Sahityashree" The Samaj, Cuttack, November 15

Saxena, N.R.S., (1987) Principles of Education, Meerut : International Publishing House.

Senapati, N.(ed.),(1971) Orissa District Gazetteers : Sambalpur. Government of Orissa

Senapati, P.M., (1963) Fakir Mohan Granthavali, Vol. I Cuttack

Shastry, V.B., (1980) Development of Secondary Education in Orissa (1882-1966), Ph. D. Education, Utkal University

Sherman, R.R., (1998) Qualitative Research in Education : Focus and Methods, London : The Falmer Press

Shrp, H, (ed.) (1908) Selections from Education Records (1781-1839), Part – I, Calcutta

Singh, S. M. S., (1995) Sahityika Drusti, Cuttack: Gaurishankar Smruti sansad

Singhdeo, J.P., (1991) Origin of Jagannath Deity, New Delhi: Gian Publishing House

Sivananda. S., (1970) Religious Education, Sivanandanagar: The Divine Life Society

Taneja, V.R., (1990)Educational Thought and Practice, New Delhi: Sterling Publishers Private Ltd.

Toynbee, G., (1960) A Sketch of History of Orissa (1803-1028) OHRJ, Vol. IX, No. 1&2

Vivekananda, S., (1994) The Ideal of Karma Yoga, Selections from the Complete Work of Swami Vivekananda, Calcutta : Advaita Ashram.

Reports Gazettees and Others

Annual Administrative Report, Bihar and Orissa, 1924-25

Annual Administrative Report, Bihar and Orissa, 1927-28

Annual Report on Newspapers, Government of Bihar and Orissa, Political Special, File No. 144 and 163 of 1921

Calcutta Gazettee Supplement, 23.10.1895

Civil Secretariat Bundle Correspondences, Political 16 of 1865, Nagpur Records. 23.10.1865

Fakir Mohan Senapati's Petition to the then Commission of the Central Provinces in 1896 collection from Regional Achieves, Orissa, Balasore, Accn. No. 72.

General Report of Public Instruction, 1852 – 55

General Report on Public Instruction in the lower Provinces of Bengal Presidency, 1857 -58

Report of the Council of Education, 1847 – 48

Report of the Council of Education, Appx – 2, 1844 – 45

Report of the General Committee of Public Instruction of Fort William i Bengal, 1839 – 40

Report of the Indian Statutory Commission, Vol. IV, 1930

Report of the Partially Excluded Areas Enquiry Committee, Orissa, Cuttack. 1940.

Reports on the State of Education in Bengal 1935 and 1938 of W. Adams, University of Calcutta, 1941.

♦♦♦

CPSIA information can be obtained
at www.ICGtesting.com
Printed in the USA
LVHW052022130323
741532LV00013B/1273

9 789743 750793